WHO AI

AN ORDINARY WOMAN
SEARCHES FOR HER IDENTITY
IN A WORLD GONE MAD.

The further adventures of Derek and Dawn,
continuing from their journey
in 'Now Everything Changes'

BY STEVE MALTZ

Saffron Planet
PO Box 2215
Ilford IG1 9TR
UK
T: +44 (0) 7885 941848
E: contact@saffronplanet.net

Copyright (c) 2024 Steve Maltz

First published 2024

The right of Steve Maltz to be identified as the Author of this Work has been asserted by him in accordance with the Copyright, Designs and Patents Act 1988.

All rights reserved. No part of this publication may be reproduced, stored in a retrieval system, or transmitted in any form or by any means, electronic, mechanical, photocopying, recording or otherwise, without the prior permission of the publisher or a licence permitting restricted copying.
In the UK such licenses are issued by the Copyright Licensing Agency, 90 Tottenham Court Road, London W1P 9HE.

ISBN 978-1-9163437-8-8

Typeset in 11/15pt Meriden by Michael Oakley
Front cover by Steve Oakley

WHO AM I?

Contents

PART ONE
Dawn's Story

INTERMISSION

PART TWO
A Matter of Identity

PART THREE
Which Kingdom?

WHO AM I?

PART ONE
Dawn's Story

1 It had been a long day already, yet it was only 2pm. If it was up to Derek, we would have been home ages ago, parked on our comfy chairs watching the telly and snoozing through Countdown. But, being an insistent lady, I demanded that we took full advantage of our day trip to MidTown market, held in the grounds of the medieval castle. This was a special occasion, a rare treat for shoppers, particularly those keen on the esoteric and quirky. The *One World, One Love* market day only came round four times a year and this was our first time. I had been keen for ages to sample its strange delights, but Derek, not known for his love of outdoors shopping (or any shopping come to think of it), had always found an excuse for not coming; flare-up of his bunions, England football game on the TV, barber's appointment. This time I had blindsided him by checking in his diary first and announcing our trip at the last minute. He was trapped and accepted defeat with grace. So here we are, Derek and Dawn Courtney, well into middle-age, rubbing shoulders with ageing hippies, fellow suburban adventurers and various hawkers and purveyors of the exotic.

Derek is well out of it and, I have to confess, I am starting to flag, my initial zeal well exhausted.

"Can we go home now?", he asks, staggering by my side with an exaggerated and probably fake limp. "Haven't we seen everything? I'm knackered."

I am tempted to agree with him. My legs are most definitely aching. He had spent most of our trip lounging on benches reading his newspaper and people-watching, while I manfully (womanfully?) pressed on, intent on sampling the fullness of

WHO AM I?

it all. I am not quite sure why. It's not an attitude I grew up with. I used to be quite content with the basics of life, all that dwelt within my comfortably small circle of influence, but not now. My recent adventures, shared with Derek, have put me on a different path, *to follow the evidence and find the truth*. It opened our eyes to the reality of antisemitism but, once opened, these aging eyes of mine will not be content with just *the ordinary*. What this means is that, in earlier times I would have finished off this market in a whistle-stop tour, only allowing the familiar to tickle my interest. Not now, I'm afraid. Now ... everything interests me. I have this thirst for knowledge that seems unquenchable. How crazy is that?

"One last circuit, Derek ... OK?" He nods, reluctantly. I move off before he changes his mind.

I argue with shamans, astrologers and fortune tellers, undaunted by their 'certainties' and enjoy the playful banter with those who are not quite so certain. I avoid the occult jewellery stands and those offering a bewildering selection of Buddhas and Hindu goddesses. There's a fine line between religiosity and tackiness I decide. None of this appeals to me and I park this realisation for later investigation as I was never quite so discerning before! *Perhaps I am changing. Interesting.*

I finally get to the point where my curiosity is overtaken by exhaustion and go looking for Derek. I had left him at a small café, nursing a huge mug of frothy coffee. As I wander back to him something catches my eye.

It was hard to miss because it was so colourful, but it was also easy to miss because it was a small stall, wedged between a vegan food van and an unkempt bush. I had not seen it earlier but now my eyes are drawn to it, as if an invisible finger hooks me in. *Perhaps there was some kind of nudge* was a thought I later

WHO AM I?

entertained when I was considering the consequences of my actions.

The name on the sign above is *RainbowGlass* and it boasts a collection of brightly coloured objects; flags, necklaces, coasters and even little bugs with spindly legs. What they all have in common is their colouring, multi-coloured stripes, all, apparently, with some sort of meaning. Also, consistent with the name, they are all made out of some kind of glass. Even the middle-aged man running the stall has a huge fluffy rainbow-striped jumper. He isn't made of glass, though perhaps a little glassy-eyed. *This is interesting*, I think, perhaps naïvely. *All variations of the rainbow, how colourful and calming.* I approach the stall and see that all of the objects have labels attached to them with instructions. Then comes the shock. I look at the coasters.

Gay Man (a green/blue pattern), A man who is attracted to a man. ***Bisexual (a red/blue pattern),*** A person who is attracted to both male and female.

Once my brain adjusts to the significance of these rainbow designs, my eye lands on these two familiar scenarios. *OK, I think. I can see where this is going.* I wasn't quite so sheltered as to be unaware of the gay community and its adoption of the rainbow image, but I wasn't expecting to see rainbow depictions for such things as *abrosexuality,* where sexuality is ever-changing, or *demiboy,* where a person partially identifies as a man. To be frank, many of the over-a-hundred varieties on display here are unprintable and should never occupy the innocent mind of a straight-forward middle-aged lady like myself! I am intrigued. I am horrified. I just don't know what to think, it is so far beyond my cosy little world. I pluck up courage and engage Mr rainbow jumper here, wondering what badge he would wear out of those on display and, more

WHO AM I?

importantly, how this would affect how I engage with him. Anyway, here goes ...

"Can I ...?"

"... ask me a question? I can see by your face that you're bursting to."

He has a surprisingly gentle, even reassuring, voice. It's as if the tone of his voice is suggesting to me, *don't worry about what you're about to hear, it's all going to be alright, there's nothing here to fear.* Maybe he practised developing this soothing tone, to deflect questions that may be thrown at him in anger?

"Perhaps you ask it, then. You seem to know what I'm about to say."

"OK, my lovely. Why so many flags? That's it, isn't it?"

"Why yes. I presume each flag says something unique, otherwise you wouldn't have created so many. Who buys them?"

"People who ... identify with the flag of course."

"But some of them ... look at this one ..."

I pointed to a coaster with a silhouette of a cat's head on a background of random stripes.

"Oh yes. Just sold one of those. It was a necklace." He looks behind me to the left. "There she goes, that lady there."

I turned round just to see a young lady in a ... cat suit would you believe, just disappearing behind a tree. She walks with a kind of ... feline grace.

"That is an extreme example," he says. "She doesn't actually think she's a cat, she just has a strong identification with them."

"Do these come in all domestic pet varieties?" I ask, playfully,

WHO AM I?

though cringing inside.

"You are taking the mickey aren't you, my lovely? But yes. Look at this one."

He picks up a coaster with diagonal stripes behind a red ... dog bone.

"Puppy pride," he says. "People dress up as puppies and play together ... in a safe environment of course."

Have I entered a parallel universe? Is this real or have I walked into a lamppost and am dreaming all of this up?

No, this man and his stall are real and his sincerity is clear to see. He absolutely believes in what he is selling. He continues.

"Everyone should be free to identify as whatever gender they feel comfortable with. We want the world to be a happy place, where people can feel included and represented."

There's a question that I'm bursting to ask, but not bold enough to do so. *Why now? Have people always been like this, but just repress it? Why are people 'coming out of the woodwork' and feeling able to identify with cats or dogs or ... well the mind boggles.* I chicken out. Instead, I ask a sensible question, one that has just popped into my mind.

"So, what about me? I'm a happily married woman ... married to a ... happily married man. Is this considered normal these days? Where do I fit into ... this?" I pointed to the display before me.

"Oh yes, we have a flag for you. Of course. The straight flag. Here it is."

He gives me a coaster that was devoid of colour, just alternating black and white stripes. From his expression you could see that he is not particularly impressed and was already losing

WHO AM I?

interest in me.

"Not very ... gay is it?" I say, then quickly correcting myself. "I mean ... gay in the traditional sense ... not very colourful. Just black and white?"

He shrugs, as if in sympathy for someone like myself, doomed to live a colourless, uncomplicated life. I actually feel he's sorry for me. I would rather turn the whole thing on its head and feel glad that my life is just ... black and white. There's certainty in black and white, a certainty that perhaps the world now frowns upon. This man certainly thinks that I've lost out in some way. He's even pursing his lips, lifting his wrists and rolling his fingers forward like a ... puppy. *Puppy pride!* I now see the badge on his jumper. I had mistaken it for a design feature. Before an unseemly giggle manifests, I quickly mouth my goodbyes and turn away, leaving him in his bubble and returning to the real world.

As I make my way back to Derek I get thinking about my place in the world. Am I a dying breed? Have I been left behind? Is it a problem to be happy and content with the way I am? Am I just stubborn and resistant? Should I not examine myself more and see if ... I am not sure where this train of thought is going. I decide to park my thoughts and, as we are prone to do, chew the cud with Derek later on, when we're back in the comfort zone of our living room with satisfying mugs of steaming hot chocolate in our hands.

2 "Do I sense a new adventure, love?" Derek seems concerned, though I can sense excitement too.

"Perhaps", I say, swirling the hot drink in my mouth. "Or perhaps ... it's just the old adventure, continued?"

"What do you mean?"

WHO AM I?

"We followed the evidence, didn't we? We followed it wherever it took us ..."

"That hill in Ulverston ... where it all started ... the Palestinian flag ... where no Palestinian flag should be?"

"Right. But I think we knew it wouldn't end there."

"I suppose so" he replies, "but it was so ... exhausting."

"Exhilarating, rather. I think you agree deep down."

"But I thought we'd have some rest first. Y'know, do a bit of gardening, start a new jigsaw ..."

"... The truth waits for no man, Derek."

"Or woman!"

"Yes. And this woman is ... ready for ... whatever."

"And?"

"Let me tell you exactly what happened to me in the market ..."

I give him a blow-by-blow account of my mini-adventure and watch his face while doing it. He is impassive but thoughtful. He is quiet for a bit as if mulling over his opening salvo before delivering it.

"So, we're black and white are we?" He pauses, then continues. "That makes us grey doesn't it? I think I'm quite content being a ... grey person. Suits me down to the ground."

"You're not a grey person, love ... you are far more than that. You don't need a colour to define you. You are ... you."

"And you are ... you."

"But ... apparently ... this is not enough for some. Perhaps this is our new adventure."

"Eh?"

WHO AM I?

"Perhaps we need to look in a mirror and ask ... Who am I?"

"Who am I?" he muses. "Now that's a question and a half."

"Or perhaps it's not a question at all? ... I don't know ... Am I going a bit weird, Derek? You would tell me, wouldn't you?"

He shrugs. I throw my slipper at him. It misses, thankfully.

"Then, my dear Dawn ... let's find out."

I smile and lean over to kiss him, leaving sloppy chocolate stains on his cheek. "That's my Derek ... he's back."

"Time for beddy byes ..."

"Race you."

Here I am, sitting in a huge, opulent lounge on an armchair so comfy that it threatens to lull me into comfortable sleep. No chance of that, though, I am so glad to be back here, having missed the last two sessions of the *Lovely Ladies Literary Loungers*. Facing me are my four fellow travellers on our adventure, four ladies who, like me, are so fascinated by the world of books that we are willing to meet weekly to chew the cud over whatever was on the table in front of us. Currently, we have been reading *Awake*, written by the author of *Zionion*, the book that was so much a part of my recent adventures into antisemitism and its implications. I secretly hope that this new journey is not going to be as fraught.

Because of my recent absence, I hadn't really had a chance to dig deeply into *Awake*. In fact, I have the book in my hands for the first time, flicking through its pages and reading snippets at random. And, frankly, I am amazed. So much so that the tingling in my spine has reappeared, nudging me back into the mindset that Derek and I were drifting into in our previous adventure, a feeling that perhaps invisible hands are guiding

WHO AM I?

me ... but we won't go there for now.

Lady Thraxton – yes, an actual lady (this being her house, helping to explain the opulence) – opens the proceedings. A rotund woman, dripping with jewellery and casual confidence, she is pleasant enough and well respected, but perhaps a little too revered by this happy little bunch.

"Well, ladies, here we are again. How marvellous. It is good to see a full complement this week. Welcome back, Dawn."

I nod at her with a smile.

"We have sipped our tea, indulged our palettes with Mavis's yummy biscuits and sit here together, books in hand, hope and expectation in our hearts. Let us begin ... Susan?"

All eyes turn to Susan Beckett, a thin wisp of a woman and one blessed with a soothing reading voice. She reads from the back cover of the book.

We currently live our lives in a place of dullness of senses and thought, where we are discouraged from exercising either. It is a world where we are urged to conform to an 'acceptable' identity but to never behave as an individual; where we are allowed to have honest opinions as long as they are 'approved' by the media; where we can voice our 'disapproval' anonymously without any comeback; where we can become excluded at the drop of a hat, simply through the drop of a tweet; where we can only have a voice if it doesn't clash with louder more insistent voices. This is like wading through treacle when we should be swimming unfettered and free. If this is a new 'progressive' environment then we must start leafing through our dictionaries for 'adjustments' and see if maybe we have joined Alice in her search for the rabbit, but in a land that has lost any sense of wonder. This is the world we have inherited. Doesn't it make you feel sad? Do we fear for future generations who may well ask us, what did you do to allow this to happen? Are we content to live in this

WHO AM I?

in-between world ... or do we need to be woken up?

There is a silence as all eyes flicker to each other, but all lips remain sealed. Lady Thraxton takes the initiative.

"Quoting from the book, *what did you do to allow this to happen?* Here's a question to kick us off. What is going to happen according to this author and what can you and I do to stop it, whatever *it* is?" This all trips off her tongue rather too eloquently. Clearly she had rehearsed this question.

"Mmm, perhaps we should read the book first to find out," offers Jane Smith, a redhead with a temper to match – if you can forgive the cliché - and a delivery that often veers towards the sarcastic, though she would term it 'being incisive'.

"Well, I've read the book in full," says the rather-bright Mavis, the biscuit-maker, smugly. "It only takes a couple of hours, perhaps a bit longer if you give yourself time to mull over the words."

She pauses.

"And?" says Jane, impatiently.

"Well ... (she often prefixed her utterances with this word, perhaps to add supposed credence) ... it's an interesting premise being offered. A bit ... revolutionary I think for us 'lovely ladies' ... we're in for a bit of a ride with this one I think."

"And?" insists Jane.

"Well ... it's all about identity, I believe."

"Identity?"

WHO AM I?

"Well … you may ask. Well … it left me with one question to ask myself. It may seem a strange one, but I know this is a safe place ladies …"

"And?" This time it is Lady Thraxton speaking. Mavis pauses, grandstanding a little.

"Who am I?"

This hits me like a sledgehammer. I repeat the words.

"Who am I?"

All eyes turn to me, as I had just blurted out these words, the same words I had uttered to Derek last night.

"Explain?" says Jane, staring at me.

So I did. I gave them the same account of my interaction in the market that I had given Derek last night. As with him, it was met with silence, but I could see the interest in their eyes.

"So, when the author talks of needing to conform to an 'acceptable' identity, are you saying he's talking about all of those badges and flags you saw, Dawn?" asks Susan, with great perception.

"That's what he seemed to believe, Susan."

"And what do you think?" added Jane.

I consider for a moment, then answer. "It doesn't seem right. Is this 'identity' thing so important? Do we all have to conform?"

"Well, it's important enough for this author to warn us that one day we're all going to be answerable for how we deal with it all."

"Good point, Mavis," says Lady Thraxton. "So, what do we all think, ladies? Is it important? Do any of us 'identify' as anything

WHO AM I?

... out of the ordinary ...?"

There's a silence.

"Come on ladies ... this is a safe place ... we all trust each other here, don't we?" she adds.

There's a further silence, quite an uncomfortable one. Then Susan speaks ...

4 We're back in that café again, where we had first met the man we'd come to know as 'Podcast Steve', one of the trio who produced the *Is There Fudge on Mars* podcast that had been so helpful to us on our earlier adventure. Why are Derek and I here? To meet Steve again, of course. He was part of our story before, perhaps he'll be part of our new story. Who knows? Only time will tell.

While we wait, I tell Derek about Susan Beckett.

"She pointed to this tiny lapel badge on her collar. I had thought it was just dress jewellery and it was, but it also had a meaning. It had two horizontal pink stripes flanking a pair of intertwined violets."

"Meaning?" Derek is confused.

"Guess."

"No idea."

"Go on ... guess. Use that clever bonce of yours ... be analytical ... you keep telling me of this skillset of yours ... 'After all, I'm an architect'." I say that last bit in a mocking voice.

"OK" he says, rubbing his chin theatrically. "Pink ... that's female, isn't it? And ... well ... two pink stripes ... let me guess ... lesbian?"

"Sapphic."

WHO AM I?

"Sapphic?"

"Same thing. But also includes bisexual, pansexual and queer women."

"Eh?"

"Don't worry about it. I don't understand it either. It's just how they define themselves."

"So why does she need to wear a badge? People never used to flaunt this sort of thing, in fact, they usually went to great lengths to keep it quiet. It used to be against the law, didn't it?"

"And this is the point." I reply, just as 'Podcast Steve' arrives.

"This is what point?" he interjects, as he sits down, a drink already in his hand. "Sounds like you've started without me."

"I was just telling Derek about a lady in my book club … oh hello, Steve, by the way." I lean over and give him a peck on the cheek. Derek shakes his hand.

"She has just come out as a lesbian. Not a great shock really, you can have an intuition about these things."

"And the point is?" says Steve, sensing there was more to come.

"She was wearing a lapel badge … Sapphic pride she called it. We were wondering why do this? Why flaunt it with a badge? Can't some things be private?"

"Ah," says Steve. "You have just brought up a massive subject." He takes a huge gulp of his coffee and then speaks.

"Let me show you something." He fiddles with his phone, does a quick Google search and brings up the page he was looking for.

"Let me quote … *You may have heard the term sapphic floating around Tiktok or even seen the sapphic flag, but are you unsure about what the term really means? Don't worry! The queer community is*

WHO AM I?

constantly becoming more inclusive and normalizing detailed ways to describe our gender or sexual identity and sapphic has become an increasingly popular umbrella term."

He pauses and waits for our response. When none is forthcoming, he continues.

"Did you hear that ... constantly becoming more inclusive and normalizing detailed ways to describe our gender or sexual identity ... do you understand what they are saying here?"

"Not really", I answer. "We're happy in our blissful ignorance I suppose ..."

"But, Dawn, our ignorance, I feel, is about to come to an end. Am I right, Steve?"

"You are right, Derek. But remember your pledge ... to follow the evidence ... like you did before? Get the bit between your teeth, eh?"

"Oh yes," Derek replies. "The madness continues?"

"Too right. Now let me explain," says Steve. "You can see that this process is not fixed, it is ever-evolving. There are well over a hundred different classifications now in the 'trans community' and it won't stop there. In fact, I doubt that it will ever stop. It's like the genie has been let out of the bottle and now is far too bloated to be shoved back in!"

"Why would that be?" I ask. "Or am I just naïve beyond belief?"

"No, there's nothing naïve about you, Dawn. You two are the sane ones, it's the world that's gone doolally!"

"So why do you say that it won't stop?"

"It's the nature of the beast, I'm afraid", he says, his voice quietening a little, as if he's about to impart a great secret, too dangerous to be overheard. He continues. "There are two ways

WHO AM I?

of looking at this, the overt way ..."

"And the covert way?" suggests Derek, revelling in his cleverness.

"Right. Let me explain." He pauses and looks at both of us in turn, as if he is still measuring us up. I must say I feel a little shudder as he does so, as if what I'm about to hear will ... change everything.

"The overt way ... the way they see it themselves and how many in the world see it is that, in the spirit of 'love and inclusion', new classifications are constantly being found so that others can be brought into the fold and 'cared for' by 'joining the family'. The problem is that this would include practices that are what we once called 'deviant' and now they are being normalised. You watch, very soon you'll see – or perhaps it's already here – paedophiles being welcomed in as a 'trans group'."

"This is awful," I say. "The very thought!" He gives us time for this to sink in.

"And this is made worse by the fact that our civil authorities and national governments give credence to the basic principles of these groups and even pass laws to protect them. And we've already seen the damage that has created, with single-sex toilets and prisons etc. I think you know what I mean here."

Derek has been thinking and tries to act as the devil's advocate. "Surely those in charge will limit the more extreme versions of this? There must be sensible people in charge ... yes?"

Steve just shrugs. I get the impression that he is passionate about this subject and, as with all zealots, there can be an unwillingness to see 'another side'. Surely there must always be another side that is answerable and open to debate? I park

WHO AM I?

that thought and entertain the idea that it would be wise for Derek and I to seek those on the 'other side' to see if it is indeed as bleak a picture as Steve has been painting. He continues.

"Then there is the ... covert side." He again stops, perhaps to give us a chance to comment. We don't. *Isn't this picture he has been painting bleak enough?* Then he continues.

"Let me continue reading from the web page ... *This term describes romantic connections and emotional bonds between queer women, non-binary and trans people, expanding the definition of inclusivity beyond traditional cisgender identities. It is used to highlight the diverse experiences of individuals within the queer community and serves as a descriptor for a range of relationships, emotions, and identities. Overall, the term sapphic promotes greater acceptance and understanding of the complex and diverse nature of human sexuality and relationships.*"

He stops. He can see the confusion on our faces. "What is your first reaction to what I've just read?"

"Confusion," says Derek. "I haven't a clue what they are talking about."

"Me neither," I add.

"Yes," says Steve. "That's the point."

He can see further confusion on our faces and continues.

"Remember when you were investigating the situation between Hamas and Israel and wondered why so many were going on anti-Israel protests. Then the penny dropped and you discovered that it was all a smokescreen for the real issue ... hatred of the Jewish people, antisemitism. Compassion for the Palestinians was just a modern manifestation of the age-old hatred of the Jews. In other words ... things are not always what they seem."

WHO AM I?

Derek and I nod as we remember our recent investigation.

"And so it is with the 'trans issue'" he says. "A deflection from the real target."

"Which is?"

"What do you think?" he says, mysteriously.

Derek and I think for a bit. I am flummoxed, to be honest, but Derek rises to the challenge.

"I think that we're the target."

"Go on ..."

"Ordinary folk, like Dawn and me ... living ordinary lives."

"Go on ..." adds Steve, nodding slightly.

"That's all, I'm afraid ... for the life of me I can't even begin to understand why."

"That's fine, Derek. You're almost there. Think about the passage I've just read. You don't have to understand the terms used or even the explanations given, just the intention behind the words."

I decide to join in. "What they are trying to say is that there is no such thing as 'normal' anymore. There are no certainties to hold on to ... is that right?"

"Perfect, Dawn. You have great intuition". Derek seems a bit miffed at this and I poke my tongue at him.

"It's part of a wider process ... a covert one as I said ... that there are no absolutes anymore. Those who promote this want nothing more than a confusion over truth. They call it post-modernism or relativism and it covers just about everything. If they can convince the world that there is no such thing as normality then they can get away with anything. The result is

WHO AM I?

… as you said, Dawn, no more certainties and … as you said, Derek … a slow death of the world that ordinary people are familiar with …"

We are appalled at the implications here. It probably shows in our faces. Also, I remind myself to look up later to see what 'relativism' and 'post-modernism' actually are. I didn't want to show my ignorance at the time.

"But why?" asks Derek. I nod at this in agreement. Why?

Then Steve says something that both disappoints us and excites us.

"That's for you two to find out."

5 On the way home in the car, I voice the one thing that has been needling me about all of this.

"What do you think of what he said?" I ask.

"Food for thought," he says. He has never been one for long conversations while driving. Men are not so good at multi-tasking, I think. Or perhaps it's just Derek. I continue.

"I like the man and he was spot on before when he guided us on the Jewish thing. Perhaps it was because it was a clear-cut issue. Very black and white. The thing is now … are we dealing with a … clear-cut issue?"

"What do you mean?"

"Well … I don't know … I think we need other points of view. He seemed a bit … extreme."

"Mmm," replies Derek, "I think the word is … nuance … it's nuance that we are looking for, a bit of context, sometimes perhaps a glimpse into the world others inhabit."

There's a silence, as he fails to continue. This seems a very clever thing to say and I need more. It never comes.

"And ...? Excuse my ignorance, Derek, but ..."

"Nuance ... shades of opinion ... it's a word that I read a lot about recently in the paper."

"Because everyone has opinions, these days?"

"Right."

"They can't all be correct in their opinions, can they? Surely that couldn't work, could it?"

Derek pauses, then switches to a new thread of thought.

"But ... I've been thinking, Dawn ... along those lines. There's someone I once knew who, I think, will be helpful."

"Go on."

Derek tells me about Joe, a software designer who he used to meet every year at these architect conventions he attended, to brush up on the latest developments. It had been going on for a few years and, although they only met once a year, there was an amazing rapport between them. They really clicked and seemed to be kindred spirits. They had much in common, in terms of outlook, even their sense of humour chimed. Then everything changed. A few years ago, Derek went to the convention and, during the first break, sought out his old friend. He found Joe in the usual place, manning the stand where he sold his software products and gave out advice. Except it wasn't Joe any more standing before him. It was Jo ... and he/she was wearing a dress. This was Derek's first contact with a transsexual and it intrigued him.

"Why didn't you tell me this at the time, Derek?" I ask.

"Didn't I? I thought I did. Perhaps you weren't listening, or maybe we didn't make a thing of it at the time. It was a long time ago ..."

I consider that as a possibility. After all those were our days of cosiness, where any potential disruption of domestic cohesion was brushed aside as irrelevant to our journey through life.

"What I didn't tell you is that we kept on meeting every year. And every year he looked slightly different, like he was adjusting to the new person he was becoming and, I must say, he was doing it with real confidence. Then he just stopped coming."

"Perhaps because the world was beginning to react to people like him and he didn't want to stand out."

"Actually no ... he seemed to revel in it and now, I believe, he ... or rather she ... I can't get my head around 'they' ... has become a bit of a spokesman ... woman, rather for the movement. She's all over the place ... giving talks, running workshops, on YouTube discussion panels, even 'Ted' Talks."

"This is interesting, Derek. But ... how can this help us now?"

"Just coming to that, dear ... we're seeing him tomorrow ... in Richmond Park."

"When did you ...?"

"I texted him just after we met with Steve. I was amazed that he had time to see us, he ... she ... is a busy person these days ... much sought after. But he's in London briefly tomorrow and says he can grant us an hour of his ... her ... can't get the hang of this ... time!"

"Wow" is all I can say. "How exciting."

 Joe ... or was it Jo ... stands up to greet us as we arrive and gives us both a hearty handshake with a grin. It is one of those grins that comes from a place of sincerity

WHO AM I?

and is in no way forced. It was the grin you would get from an old acquaintance.

"Weren't expecting that were you?"

"No," says Derek, "but you always had a firm grip." I just smile nervously, a bit taken aback by his ... her appearance. I have decided to take the position of least resistance and will refer to Jo-Joe as a 'her'. She is small and a little portly, with thick masculine arms and a strong male face. Also, her voice is decidedly masculine, in fact, more manly than most men I know, which I can't help but find, mildly amusing. Balancing this, she wears a dress, a plain green affair, down to her mid-calves, finished off with flashy pink boots. Also, her hair is long and straggly and I see no sign of makeup. This is evidently a person at ease with herself, despite the confusion she may give to others!

"And this is your wife?"

"Yes, Dawn."

"Nice to meet you, Dawn. Am I as expected?"

"Umm, no ..."

"Jo. Call me Jo ... or Joe ... doesn't matter really, just both sides of the same coin really. If people call me Jo with or without the 'e' or even Jo-Joe, then no-one's offended."

"Just confused," says Derek, light-heartedly.

"And," adds Jo, "everyone's offended these days, aren't they ... so ... does it really matter anyway?"

Derek is suddenly thoughtful. "Do you get offended?" he asks.

"Oh, God no," responds Jo immediately. "I used to, but what's the point now. No one wins, do they?"

WHO AM I?

The conversation is starting to flow a lot easier than I had feared it would. I am still silent, easing into the situation after the initial shock. I am warming to Jo and feel proud of myself in the process. She senses my general unease and tells us her story, to set out her stall, so to speak.

"When I was born, believe it or not, the doctors couldn't figure out what sex I was ... I will spare you the sordid details. After an hour or so, they opted eventually for male and I was brought up as a boy in, I must say, a happy supportive environment. It never felt right, I was just as happy with Barbie as Action Man, but kept this a secret from my parents. At high school – a boy's school by the way – I was the girly, wimpy one. Hated sports, especially hated the showers after sports. Puberty came very late for me, I stood out and, unsurprisingly was bullied."

I can tell that she had recounted this tale many times as this seemed like a rehearsed performance and there was little emotion here. The scars must have healed, I guessed, quite rightly, because the worst was to come. She continues.

"I knew I wasn't right, the old cliché of a woman trapped in a man's body. I went to a psychiatrist and was diagnosed with gender dysphoria, an actual condition, unlike a lot that we see these days. It wasn't a 'fashion accessory'. Actually ... it was something of a relief to have an 'actual' condition, not an 'imagined one' ... but we won't go there ... yet. I was put on a course of hormones, oestrogen, and grew these lovely melons!"

She points to her breasts. Derek reddens and looks away. I, however, gaze at them, quite impressed and jealous at what I see. This amuses Jo, who adds, "And it didn't end there."

She finishes her story of the difficult journey she endured, culminating in the surgery of her "man-bits", basically turning them inside out, but sparing us the gory detail.

WHO AM I?

"And once I had recovered from the surgery, everything suddenly felt balanced. My gender dysphoria was no more. I felt complete."

She has finished and is keen for our reaction because it is not often - as she told us afterwards - that she has a neutral, impartial audience instead of having to defend herself against those who had already made their mind up against her ... 'and her sort'. Derek has the first question.

"So, how would you describe yourself, Joe, if you don't mind me asking?"

"I am me, Derek. I hate classifications. I hate these artificial groupings."

I decide to speak, finally. It's a rehearsed question.

"Yes, I can see that. But, in terms of the 'community' out there, how do they see you ... and how do you react to it?"

"Great question, Dawn." She continues, "Firstly ... despite appearances ... and despite common attitudes of the 'trans' community ... I am still ... male."

We are taken aback by this, so used to the perceived, militancy of the trans community, insisting that they identify with the sex they had adopted.

"I can see this surprised you. Look, you two, I was born a male ... though in my case there was a degree of confusion ... but this is fixed ... it's coded into my chromosomes and will never change ... my 23rd chromosome has one X and one Y ... whatever that actually means. But what it actually means in everyday life is that, whatever I do to my body and whatever I say about my gender, it is never going to change."

"And what about your gender?" I ask.

WHO AM I?

"A totally different thing. I consider myself a trans ... person. I could call myself a trans woman but that can confuse. Let's get this clear ... despite what Labour politicians and most of the media say ... a trans woman is still a man ... let's not confuse sex and gender."

There's a pause while we try to take this in. This seems like a significant statement, delivered with passion and certainty. Derek speaks.

"So ... your sex is male ... but your gender ... or ... the way that you feel subjectively ... is female."

"Correct ... now go out there and tell everyone else! People just don't get it or don't want to get it. There's a plague of confusion out there with people transitioning willy-nilly ... actually that's a good expression to use, must remember that ... thinking they have become something different but ... in most cases ... it's just in their mind, peer pressure, fashion."

"I bet you're not very popular for saying these things, Jo", I say, with a sudden understanding.

"Too right. Everyone hates me, I get it from both sides ... and all I am being is myself ... Jo-Joe ... that's my identity, I refuse to inhabit the artificial spaces they want to bury me in."

She speaks with great passion and I am filled with such compassion for her. Against all my basic middle-class instincts and nature, I suddenly rush forward and give her a big hug. *How so unlike me!* They are both surprised, but I see the tears in Jo's eyes. I guess that all she desires is acceptance for being ... herself. She mouths a 'thank you' to me as we embrace. Derek is moved but remains in his seat, a little embarrassed. He speaks, seemingly oblivious to all the touchy-feely stuff.

"Identity ... that's at the core of it all, I think." "But I'm not

WHO AM I?

sure how," he adds.

"You're correct, Derek," says Jo. "Look at the crazy situation with pronouns. You'd think that misgendering ... not using the 'approved' pronouns ... is a crime against humanity."

"What are your ... pronouns ... if you don't mind me asking?" I ask.

"Call me what you like ... anything except 'it' ... I answer to 'them/they' as well as 'she/her' and also 'he/him'. They are only words."

"Then why are they so important to others?"

"It's that word again ... identity ... it's been drummed into some people that their self-designed 'identity' is the most important thing in the world, even more so than how they function as a human being ... I tell you, if I were in charge, I would abolish it all and we just 'identify' as human beings, no victim groups, hierarchies, or division."

I am impressed.

"Jo," I say, "I think you are probably way ahead of your time ..."

"Or, perhaps, a throwback to better days," she adds, in a quieter voice.

7 The next meeting of the Lovely Ladies Literary Loungers is a feisty one. This is the fault of Lady Thraxton, endowed with a great deal of wealth and material advantages but sadly lacking in the common sense and empathy departments. The tone is set when, once all the niceties are through, she asks Susan a direct question.

"Why didn't you tell us earlier about your ... inclinations. Really bad form, Susan."

Susan was stuck for an answer to such a direct, personal

WHO AM I?

question. Jane, swiftly coming to her defence, has a riposte.

"Lady Thraxton … last time we were here you declared that this is a safe place. People in safe places don't judge each other."

The others nod, as do I. It is a good remark and I was proud of the usually aggressive and insensitive Jane for making it. Lady Thraxton is silent, perhaps considering her options. Attack or defence? Self-justification or contrition? Thankfully she goes for the latter.

"Mea culpa, ladies. I was being … out of order, as you say. Bad form … (and she points to herself) … moi!"

This makes us smile in relief, though Susan hasn't moved a muscle yet, as if paralysed. All eyes turn to her. Suddenly she blinks and relaxes, with a faint smile. I speak up.

"It was very brave of Susan to show such honesty. These days such things shouldn't shock us and I'm certainly not judging but … I have a question."

There's another silence as Susan finally nods at me.

"Your badge, as you said, defines you as sapphic … my question is … why wear anything at all? Why call yourself anything? We didn't used to have to belong to some … grouping. Why not just be … yourself?"

I am clearly influenced by my conversation with Jo yesterday. As someone who probably could have sported a whole swathe of badges, all Jo wanted was to be herself and to be left alone. Susan answers.

"I don't know … it seemed to be the easy option … perhaps by identifying with a group there is protection in numbers, of being part of something. I suppose I half-expect people to get who I am through my badge … and leave me alone. That was

WHO AM I?

my original thinking ... now I'm not so sure."

"Then, Susan," I say. "You're not like others who wear these badges and flags. They do so out of what they call ... pride ... they are happy to flaunt it."

"I realise that now", she answers, "but ..."

Mavis interrupts. "I don't think that 'pride' is necessarily a good thing. The book ..."

"Ah, the book", declares Lady Thraxton, holding up her copy of *Awake*. "Let's talk about the book. Mavis, you told us last week that you'd read it all. Is there anything there that can shed light into ..."

She trails off, mindful of not being inappropriate, expecting Mavis to finish her sentence. Which she does, eventually, after flicking through the pages, thumbing through coloured tags placed on some pages. She reads from the book.

"In light of all of this let's return to the question posed earlier. Do we think for ourselves? Do we allow others to control us or are we free always to operate independently? Are we secure in our identity or have we allowed others to herd us into artificial victim groups to silence our individual voices? It is time to consider our identity, in its most basic sense."

She stops reading and adds some comments of her own.

"Well, I've given this a lot of thought. And it is, frankly, ladies, quite troubling. Everyone ... it seems ... wants to belong to some group or other ... and ..."

Jane interrupts, "But ... sorry to interrupt, Mavis ... Susan here felt that being in a group gave her some sort of protection or acceptance. So ... perhaps ... it's not such a bad thing? "

Susan says, "I did ... but, to be honest ... I wish I didn't. In fact,

WHO AM I?

I really shouldn't be wearing it ..."

She ostentatiously takes off the badge, looks at it with a frown and places it in her pocket. This is puzzling, but she goes on to explain herself.

"I began to attract attention from ... let's say ... people who I wouldn't normally want to attract attention from. It wasn't a comfortable feeling, you know. Look ladies ... look at me ... I'm just a middle-aged lady who has started having feelings for ..."

"... other middle-aged ladies" added Jane, with a smile. This quip helps to relax the atmosphere. Even Susan gives a chuckle.

"Right ... but don't any of you here get any ideas. You're not my type."

"Thank goodness for that," says Lady Thraxton. "Life's already so complicated." She didn't mean this as a joke and was puzzled why we were all grinning. Susan continues.

"It was like being a freemason or something ... a secret club, a cult even. And I didn't like it ... you don't know the relief I have now ... I actually feel quite free, liberated even."

Jane leaves her seat and walks over to Susan. "Group hug", she declares. All of us take part, some with more gusto than others. It seems like a significant event in the short life of the 'Lovely Ladies'. Perhaps we really are lovely ladies? Lady Thraxton seems positively embarrassed.

"Now, ladies," she declares. "The book? I believe Mavis is still enlightening us."

Mavis speaks. "Well ... 'It is time to consider our identity'. It's what the book says. I've been thinking about my identity ..."

My ears cock up at this and there is a sudden silence. Someone else is considering the same things as Derek and I. This is

WHO AM I?

interesting. She continues.

"Susan has bravely declared herself as a ... lesbian ... can I say this word?" All nod.

"And the world has said to her ... yes, you're a lesbian ... you are defined by it ... wear the badge, fly the flag ... and expect everyone else to celebrate you ... that's what 'pride' is all about ... But ...why should we?"

"Why should we what?" asks Lady Thraxton, not quite following.

"Why should we be defined by it?" says Mavis. Susan takes over the conversation.

"So right, Mavis. Well spoken. As you know, I'm a pharmacist and I love my job and I'm good at it. When people ask me who I am I say ... I'm Susan, a pharmacist ... But, what 'these people' want me to say instead is ... I'm Susan, a lesbian ... who is also a pharmacist. My ... identity ... is what I want it to be and how the world sees me ... as a pharmacist. My sexual preferences are my affair."

Susan has built herself up into a bit of a state. There's some anger and resentment there and this concerns me. This is perhaps a more emotive subject than I realised, even after that frank discussion with Jo. There is a silence as we absorb this outburst and contemplate our reaction to it. Mavis is the first to speak.

"Yes, Susan. That is the thrust of the book. Let me read another passage. ... *We all come in a variety of shapes and sizes, inclinations, varieties, and preferences, determined either by nature or nurture. The end product of this is how the world sees us but is not necessarily our identity. We may have sexual preferences outside the norm, we may have been born into a family following a set of beliefs, we may have physical*

WHO AM I?

handicaps, and the list goes on. What our culture wants to do is to filter you into groups that share these characteristics, so that they can speak up for you ... and control you. It wants you to be defined by the group you have been placed into, it wants this to become your identity. It wants you to be a victim so that others can be blamed for your predicament (if you are a group traditionally marginalized or persecuted by society) or so that others can be castigated for not celebrating your new status."

This all reminds me of my interaction at the market stall, with that incredible array of badges and flags. I decide not to bring it up again.

8 "So we spoke of all those different identity flags and badges and Susan actually threw hers away."

I am reporting back to Derek, my 'partner in crime' at the end of the day, from the comfort of our armchairs.

"Good for her," he says.

"We don't need all of these groups to define us, do we?" I need reassurance here.

"No, my darling wife ... but ... if you had a choice, what group would you be a part of?"

He is being facetious of course, but I go along with it, as sometimes things are so ridiculous that the only response is to lighten things up.

"I think I'll create my own group. One that fits my 'identity' ... our identity."

"Yes?"

I pause to think. "Still thinking" I declare. Then I get an idea.

"It would be a pale blue background ... because I like the colour. Instead of stripes, I'll have wavy lines ... that will be my little rebellion against our 'invisible masters' who make this whole

34

WHO AM I?

thing up. They will be in black and white of course, because that's us ... black and white. And ... on top of the whole thing will be ... two dinosaur heads."

He laughs. "Dinosaur heads?"

"That's us ... prehistoric ... just where I think we'd want to be."

"Very good," he declares, "any room for a couple of mugs of hot chocolate on the flag?"

"Sorry, no."

"Never mind ... we'll survive."

"But the dinosaurs didn't!"

We stop to think hard over that remark, made in jest but, in the current climate, perhaps with a ring of truth about it.

I had a fretful sleep that night. So did Derek it seems, as, at one point he was so restless that he actually fell out of bed, landing in the laundry basket, which thankfully softened his fall. We laughed about it afterwards over breakfast but neither of us brought up our anxieties. I think we needed a bit of rest from it all.

That rest was broken by a strange sound from outside. It sounded like a radio blaring from someone's front garden. But it was only eight o'clock in the morning and this was normally a quiet neighbourhood. People just don't do that sort of thing around here, we are considerate people.

"You hear that?" says Derek. I nod. He seems unconcerned and returns to his daily paper and toast fingers.

"I suppose it's up to me, as usual", I mumble, walking over to the front door. I open it and step outside. There's a sound wafting through the air. It's a man's voice, chanting something incomprehensible. It seems to be everywhere, but the source is further down the main road, just around the corner. I decide to investigate. "Just popping out for a bit," I cry. There's a grunt in return. I roll my eyes and leave the house, walking towards the main road.

It's a Sunday and there are not many people about. Those who are seem oblivious to the sound, or perhaps they hadn't fully woken up yet. I pop into the service station opposite, where we buy our daily papers.

"Do you hear that?" I ask Gul, the always-smiling Sikh lady working behind the counter.

"Yes, I do, Dawn. They've been at it since I got here an hour ago."

"At it? Who?"

"The Muslims," she says, with frustration and a little anger in her voice.

"The Muslims?"

"Yeah, it's their call to prayer." She raises her voice a little. "Isn't it, Abid?"

Abid, the young Muslim sitting behind her answers. "It's coming up to Eid. It's the Athan ... or Adhan ... the call to prayer."

"Yeah ... but in NewTown ... England?" says Gul, with the veiled venom of an English patriot.

Abid seems embarrassed at this. Just shrugs his shoulders and carries on serving a customer. Gul looks at me in exasperation.

"They're taking over, y'know."

I had no answer to that. I can see where this is coming from. The sound of Islamic chanting somehow doesn't fit in with

WHO AM I?

English suburbia on a quiet Sunday morning. Church bells, yes, but a strange strident tongue … I don't think so. Yet, I don't want to sink to the levels of a racist and it certainly seems weird for a Sikh to be voicing such concerns. There's a lot to tell Derek, or perhaps I'll hold back a bit, in case he reacts in a way that may embarrass himself. One just doesn't know, does one?

I return to Derek and sit down opposite him. He looks up from his paper.

"OK? Can still hear the radio," he mutters, oblivious to my mini-adventure.

"More tea?" I ask. He nods and I leave the table.

And so we took a welcome rest from it all. For nearly a week we just got on with our lives with not a mention of our latest adventure. Instead, we busied ourselves with our pastimes, me with my ongoing battles with my garden and Derek with his hobby electronics, an attempt to rediscover the sense of wonder he had as an adolescent, battling with transistors and resistors and failing to get anything to work, due to his clumsiness. Yet it brought back a positive nostalgia and he now found that he was able to create projects that actually worked when switched on. This included a home-built computer that functioned the first time he powered it up, causing him to jig around in delight. His pride and joy, though he had actually no use for a computer these days. His iPhone now provides for all of his technological needs.

In fact, during this time, we barely spoke at all, just the bare minimum, enough to keep a comfortably secure marriage going. Each was alone in their thoughts. All this was to change, however, after the next meeting of the Lovely Ladies Literary Loungers.

WHO AM I?

"So what do we make of the book, ladies, now that we have been dissecting it for a few weeks?" This is Lady Thraxton speaking. Evidently, she had now finally finished reading it and is speaking out of confidence with her usual superior air.

"Well ...", says Mavis. "I've now read the book twice over ..."

Lady Thraxton rolls her eyes at that. Mavis continues. "I think perhaps I can read the summary and we can comment if we ... have come to the same conclusions as the author ... perhaps?"

"Good idea," says Jane. "Read on."

"Here's an interesting passage," says Mavis. *We are all individuals. Although we may intentionally find identity in groups of like-minded people, this has to be balanced against a false identity that has been foisted upon us in the form of 'victim groups'. This devalues us as individuals and stops us from wanting to be better people and being truly independent thinkers, rather than being dictated to by others. We need to be secure in who we are, rather than what others tell us."*

After a short period of cogitation, Mavis speaks again.

"It's strange ... isn't it?" She stops as everyone stares at her, urging her to get on with it. Jane even makes some hand movements to express the group's frustration.

Mavis finally continues. "It's strange that we can even be talking about such a thing. It's what we said last week ... why can't everyone accept who we all are ... ordinary human beings just doing our best to be ourselves?"

I agree with this and develop her argument. "Right, Mavis. You know, when Derek and I talked about my visit to that market stall and saw all of the flags and the groups they represented, the question I put to him was this ... Who am I? Why should I even be asking this question?"

38

WHO AM I?

"We used to just get on with things", adds Jane.

"Keep calm … and carry on", says Lady Thraxton, "Like we did in wartime."

Wartime? How old was Lady Thraxton? She was definitely old-school but certainly not old enough to be dodging doodlebugs, though I suspect that if she had lived through the war it would have been in the comfort of her country house in the Cotswolds, with servants flapping around her and business as usual. I chuckle at the mental image.

Susan, who had been very quiet up to this point, replies.

"I have given this a lot of thought, ladies. This book has helped me to think through things about, about … y'know."

We knew.

"I can see the need to be open about ourselves", she adds. "In the past, it was all swept under the carpet, wasn't it?"

"Had to be, it was against the law", says the always-direct Jane, adding "I'm sorry for my bluntness by the way."

"Let's not go there," I say, "one of the positive developments of the openness we have is that we have learned to accept one another."

"But perhaps we have taken it too far", adds Mavis, "as the book explains. These 'victim groups', I ask you. In the old days perhaps we would have labelled them as eccentricities or anomalies … or am I being a bit crass here?"

"Maybe, Mavis," says Jane, "but I get your drift. I think we need to hear more from Susan. Hope we haven't offended you, girl?"

"No, I'm fine" says Susan, and you can see she means it. She continues. "I accept that I'm different but … I don't see the

WHO AM I?

need to ... celebrate it."

"Yes," says Lady Thraxton. We are hoping that her next words are going to be from a place of sensitivity rather than the usual bluster.

"And what's this whole 'Pride' thing about anyway? I see we've just come out of a whole month of it. The media has been full of it. The other day I saw a sign on the door of the local Tesco, 'Standing Proud Together' it said. That had been up there for a full month! Wouldn't a day have been enough?"

She is quite flustered and you can see that this is a bit of an issue for her. My issue – facetious as it was – was that surely the Lady would rather eat glass than admit to shopping at Tesco! She continues.

"We don't see people like us being ... celebrated like this do we?"

"Would we want to?" asks Jane, smiling.

"No, but that's not the point. Isn't it all a bit ... over the top?"

I agree with Lady Thraxton, but probably wouldn't have expressed it quite so forcefully. Susan speaks next. "Actually, you are right, Lady Thraxton. We need to find a balance, between acceptance and ... celebration."

"And who makes the rules up anyway?" asks Jane.

We have no answer to this and it really makes us think.

"Yes ..." says Mavis. "How did it get like this? We live in a world where we are all so scared to speak out of place in case we offend someone. I know this is a safe space but ... Susan ... I feel more worried about offending you than anything else ... why should it be so?"

"And of course, people are now being ... what's the word ... *cancelled* ... for things they may have said or written or done

WHO AM I?

yonks ago" adds Lady Thraxton, with concern mixed with frustration etched on her face.

Suddenly, something clicks within my head, a connection with my previous adventure. When Derek and I were investigating antisemitism and its sources we saw how influential the ideas from the far left had created such a poisonous toxic culture that it allowed hate to take root and begin to thrive. Marxism was the key driver and, perhaps, what we see here is the same source. *Why am I having such deep thoughts? Dare I bring it up? What if I am wrong?* In the end, it didn't matter, because Susan speaks up.

"I've been looking into the subject," she says. "This whole 'pride' thing that I had bought into with that badge. It's just manipulation as far as I can see. I feel that I and others like me are just being exploited … and so I asked myself … who would want to do this? Then I watched a video by Jordan Peterson …"

"Isn't he the one who hates women?" says Jane.

"No … I don't think so," replies Susan. "Just because he directs a lot of his talks towards empowering men, it doesn't mean he hates women …" She pauses, then adds, " …I think."

"Best not condemn someone out of hand," I say. "I think a lot of people say a lot of things about this man but, until we hear him for ourselves …"

"That's right," interrupts Susan. "I have and … he's OK I think … and he talks about the 'pride' thing and the 'victim culture' and … he talks about the influence of *Marxism*."

"Marxism?" says Lady Thraxton.

Marxism? I think to myself … *how interesting.*

WHO AM I?

"You mean communists and the like?" Lady Thraxton continues. "Thought they were long gone."

"And, of course, the book we've been reading says the same thing" adds Mavis.

"Oh does it?" says Lady Thraxton, embarrassed, realising that her reading of it wasn't as thorough as she had thought.

Mavis flicks through her well-worn copy of *Awake* and reads from it.

"The rise of victim groups is, as we saw, a modern phenomenon, but it didn't just come out of nowhere. It's a manifestation of the critical theory proposed by those Marxist disrupters many years ago and its sole aim is to screw us all up! And has it succeeded? I would say 'yes'."

"Ah ... those Marxists" says Lady Thraxton, "Now I remember ... those Krauts a hundred years ago ... nothing good ever comes from that damn country."

This is met by silence. It was an unwritten rule that we wouldn't act in any prejudicial manner against any population group and, it seems, this has been broken for the first time. *Thankfully no one here has German ancestry*, I think.

I break the awkward silence. "So much to ponder on here."

They nod in agreement.

"I think it's coffee time, ladies," exclaims Lady Thraxton, eager to deflect. "And I believe Susan has made one of her yummy sponge cakes."

This breaks the mood, which disappoints me, but I can see that the official part of the meeting has come to a premature end. Except for myself and, possibly Mavis, judging by the expression on her face, most are relieved to lighten the atmosphere.

Yes, I say again to myself this time. *Much to consider.*

WHO AM I ?

10 After giving Derek a thorough run-down of the book club meeting we decided that this would be a good time to renew our acquaintance with 'Podcast Steve'. I know that I've come a long way since our last meeting and feel that our next meeting could be more of a conversation between (almost) equals rather than a lecture, as it was before.

So here we are in the café, with half-drunk coffees in front of us as we bring Steve up-to-date. He's impressed, particularly regarding our enlightening meeting with Jo-Joe a few days earlier. It seems that even Steve had new things to learn on some fronts.

"You have done us all a service, I think. I wouldn't have dreamed of engaging with a hardened trans woman, I'm far too much of a coward," he says.

"Trans person ... not woman", I remind him. "Jo is adamant about this ... ultimately he sees himself as just a person ... and he ... she ... is not exactly 'hardened' ... quite soft and gentle really ..."

"... but one on an extraordinary journey" adds Derek.

"... and certainly not 'hardened'" he agrees, "quite a soft centre I think."

"Quite, "agrees Steve. "I would love to meet him ... her."

"I think 'they' prefer 'them'" I add with a grin.

"Pronouns!" Steve explains, "Why, oh why. Oh why?"

"Is that a new pronoun, Steve?" jokes Derek. "Y O Y O Y? Yoyoy? Rather like the sound of that one. Ideal, perhaps, for someone thoroughly fed up with the whole business and wants the world to know it?"

WHO AM I?

We groan for a bit and then some silence ... for a bit. Steve then faces me and asks me a direct question, "Dawn ... what do you think you have learned on this journey of yours, so far? Derek, feel free to comment too."

I compose myself, then speak.

"It started with those flags, supposedly all linked to gender 'identities'. My friend Susan was wearing one but suddenly realised that she didn't need to. You told us, Steve, in the last meeting that, in reality, this whole thing has been manufactured just to sow confusion ... I wasn't so sure about it when you said this until ... I saw the confusion in Susan's face. It was almost the same with Jo, someone who has seen this 'movement' grow around her but has remained her own person ... and has been persecuted from both sides by doing so."

Derek speaks. "And Jo agreed with you, Steve ... it's just about confusion."

I continue. "Yes ... but Jo refused to become a victim ... she refuses to be categorised ... just wants to be ... herself."

"And wants to have her own identity ... not one dictated by others," adds Derek.

I continue the story. "So Susan threw away her badge ... and she made this wonderful declaration. I wrote it down ..." I read from my trusty notebook.

As you know, I'm a pharmacist and I love my job and I'm good at it. When people ask me who I am I say ... I'm Susan, a pharmacist ... But, what 'these people' want me to say instead is ... I'm Susan, a lesbian ... who is also a pharmacist. My ... identity ... is what I want it to be and how the world sees me ... as a pharmacist. My sexual preferences are my affair!

WHO AM I?

I finish my account. "It seems that this is all a Marxist conspiracy. Is this true, Steve?"

He isn't expecting this. "Whoa," he says. "Slow down!" Another pause, then Steve says, "Actually you're right ... but, before you go there, there's something I want to show you."

He taps away at his iPad and swings it around so that it faces us. He starts up a video.

"It's only about a minute and a half. Watch it first, then we'll talk about it."

It is a YouTube video of London Pride 2024, compiled by *The Independent* newspaper. We watch it as he watches us. True enough, it only lasted around ninety seconds.

"First impressions?" he asks.

"Colourful", says Derek. "And noisy," I add.

"Are they having a good time?" Steve asks.

"You can say that. Lots of smiling faces. So many costumes."

"Amused by the Navy and Army marching to YMCA," adds Derek, attempting some half-remembered hand gestures learnt at many a disco in the (supposedly) innocent 1970s.

"But pretty harmless," I conclude. "Yes?"

Steve gathers himself. Evidently, he disagrees. He speaks.

"Do you remember that march you went to all of those weeks ago, Derek? The pro-Palestinian one?"

"How can I forget?"

"Can you see the contrast?"

"Yes ... snarling faces and messages of hate ... against the smiling faces and messages of love that we see here."

WHO AM I?

"Good observation ..." says Steve.

Then he says something that actually shocks me.

"... but two sides of the same coin."

Derek is also shocked. "Explain."

Steve continues. "In both cases, you have huge groups of people – mostly young people you've probably observed – all united in a single cause. One was – as we discovered – a corporate expression of hate ... for Israel and the Jews ... and the other ... here ... is a corporate expression of love ... or so it seems."

Now it's my turn. "Explain."

Steve continues. "Well ... I'm not sure if you noticed ... how comfortable would you be at a carnival where Durex had a float featuring a schoolgirl and a devil figure, and the crowd is full of people wearing fetish uniforms?"

"Don't even know what that is."

"Dressing up ... in a questionable manner. Use your imagination!"

"Oh, OK."

"Returning to my ... theme ... in both cases people are supporting a cause, are cementing their identity to this cause ... yet both causes are highly questionable."

Derek says, "Yes, I understand you on the pro-Palestine march but ... this lot here ... isn't it just innocent fun?"

"Not innocent, believe me ... I can show you other stuff from the march that will make you feel very ill indeed ... including a life-size effigy of Jesus as a gay black man!" He visibly shivers as he says this.

He's silent now as we take this in. I can imagine how Christians

WHO AM I?

would feel about this, though the 'black' element is just a curious touch rather than offensive I would think. However, it still made me a little uneasy for some reason. He speaks again.

"Think about the whole concept, this 'Pride' thing. Whatever you may feel about LGBT, the thought that not only should we celebrate it, but that society would *be expected to celebrate it,* even the corporate world during 'Pride Month' ... it smacks of manipulation to me, doesn't it?"

I'm about to answer when I hear a beep from my pocket. I fiddle with my phone and notice a WhatsApp message. It is from the Lovely Ladies. That's strange, it's very rare to get any communications from the group at all. I am intrigued and I open it.

Extraordinary meeting tomorrow at 7:30pm ladies. Please try and make it. Lady T.

11 We are all here. Of course we are. We don't often – ever - have 'extraordinary meetings'. I am hoping that there are positive reasons for this sudden gathering rather than bad news. We are about to find out as Lady Thraxton makes her usual grand entrance, but perhaps without the usual flourish. This time she has two ladies in tow, who meekly follow her and sit down either side of her. Lady Thraxton has a smile on her face, but it is a very weak one. She seems uncomfortable.

"Let me introduce our two new members, ladies."

She gestures to the lady on her left. A rather rotund black lady, dressed in jeans and a big floppy brightly coloured sweatshirt, with a dazzling smile that lights up her face. She seems to be really pleased to be here. *She's going to liven us up, I wonder what the others think?*

WHO AM I?

"Give a big welcome to Dolores Carter", says Lady Thraxton, with a voice that could be a little more welcoming. I detect unease, perhaps a tinge of upper-class racism here, though that particular thought was held way back in the grimy depths of my mind and left there. Dolores nods and speaks, addressing us all in turn.

"It is such a pleasure for me to be here. I look forward to getting to know you all better."

We also smile and give her a gentle clap. Lady Thraxton now turns to the lady on her right. This lady couldn't have been more different to Dolores. She is small and frail looking, barely filling her green, delicately adorned sari, with a quiet nervous disposition. You can see that she is trying to smile, but her jaw muscles strain to no avail.

"And also welcome …" Lady Thraxton peers at a scrap of paper in her hand. "… Sunita Alahan," still with not the most welcoming tone in her voice. Sunita relaxes just a little and nods very faintly. She says nothing, evidently a shy person. We give her a welcoming clap.

Lady Thraxton interrupts. "No time to waste … and now on to business … Mavis, can you bring the ladies up to date as to our current book?"

Mavis grabs two books from the coffee table by her side and gives them to the two ladies. Dolores puts hers on her lap, while Sunita eagerly grabs hers and flicks through the pages. Mavis launches into her summary.

"Well … we've been looking through the book and made some observations already … not sure if I can do it justice really … um …"

It is clear that she is struggling, so I help out.

WHO AM I?

"I hope you don't mind, Mavis ... I think ... ladies ... that we can summarise everything in a single word ... 'identity'. Do we agree?"

There is some general nodding. Mavis blusters a bit. "Well ... it's a bit more complicated than that, but ... I suppose ..."

Jane interrupts. "Got it in one, Dawn. Identity. Susan ... you summarised it well. Can you remember what you said?"

Susan is silent so I jump in. "I wrote down what she said. Is it OK if I repeat it now, Susan?"

She nods, evidently both relieved and impressed that her words were worth recording. Again, I read from my trusty notebook.

As you know, I'm a pharmacist and I love my job and I'm good at it. When people ask me who I am I say ... I'm Susan, a pharmacist ... But, what 'these people' want me to say instead is ... I'm Susan, a lesbian ... who is also a pharmacist. My ... identity ... is what I want it to be and how the world sees me ... as a pharmacist. My sexual preferences are my affair!

Susan smiles and nods her head. Lady Thraxton interrupts.

"Any questions or comments, ladies?" She is speaking to the two new members. Sunita immediately shakes her head and stays silent. Dolores is not so silent.

"And I'm a proud black woman and I don't care who knows it. And as far as what goes on in my bed chamber ... you can dream on 'cos I ain't telling."

She collapses into guffaws of laughter before noticing that no one else is following her cue. Suddenly Jane bursts into laughter. She had been suppressing it, waiting for everyone else's reaction but could do it no longer. I am very thankful for this, a real ice-breaker. I smile as does Susan. The other two

WHO AM I?

remain stony-faced and poor old Sunita doesn't seem to get it at all.

"Well …", says Mavis, her voice a little quieter than usual. There is also a sternness about it. "Let's have a bit of decorum here."

Lady Thraxton seems to agree, judging by her body language. Dolores is unfazed.

"Looks like the Good Lord has sent me here to shake some life into you." At that she gives a smile as broad as her face and I can't help but smile back.

"You are a bit … lively for us … old-fashioned folk."

"Nothing wrong with a bit of life, dearie. Life is for living and laughing. Living and laughing …"

She looks at Mavis.

"Looks like you can do with a bit of … living and laughing … come on … give us a smile."

Mavis will have none of that. She clearly sees this as some kind of veiled attack.

"Well …", she said. "Well …"

Two 'wells'? I thought. *This isn't good.*

It wasn't, because Mavis immediately got to her feet, grabbed her book and her coat and left the room without a single comment.

We are stunned. Dolores not so much.

"Was it something I said?" she asks, innocently, only slightly smiling now.

I leave the room and hurry after Mavis. I catch her up by the front door, actually about to leave.

WHO AM I?

"Mavis!" I shout. She turns round for a moment, is about to speak, then changes her mind and opens the door and leaves. I follow her. I am determined not to let her go without explanation.

"Mavis!" I shout again.

This time she stops but doesn't turn around. I approach her and coax her to a garden bench, where we both sit down. Her head hangs down, her hands are in her lap. She seems disconsolate. Eventually she speaks.

"I could kick myself ... kick myself ..." She looks up. I am puzzled.

"What do you mean, Mavis? Hey, it's OK, take your time."

She gathers her thoughts, looks around to make sure there's no one else about and then speaks.

"Between you and me, Dawn ..."

"Yes?"

"I ... am ..."

She struggles to get the rest out. I am patient and encourage her by showing as much concern as I can muster in my face. There's silence for a few seconds. Her lower lip is trembling. Tears are forming. *This must be big,* I thought. It was.

"I ... am ... a ... disgusting ... racist."

Well, that is unexpected. I try not to show it but fail. She picks up on this.

"There ... see ... even you are disgusted with me."

"No, I'm not, Mavis. Just a little shocked ... a bit unexpected." This is the truth. Meek and mild Mavis surely has not got a racist bone in her body? Yet ... *there's nowt so strange as folk,* as

WHO AM I?

the old Yorkshire – I think - saying goes.

She sighs. Her expression softens. "I suppose ..."

"You're not a racist, Mavis. I've known you for some time ... I would have known."

"That's the point, Dawn. I've hidden it well. Until ..."

"Dolores?"

"Yes", she admits, meekly. "I couldn't cope with what she said. It was as if she could read into my soul ... and tried to mock me."

"No, no, no. She was joking. Granted she could have been a bit more subtle, but I guess that's her way."

Mavis considers this for a bit. "I haven't really met ... anyone like Dolores before."

"And that's the point, Mavis. Probably none of us has, that's how insulated we've been! That doesn't make you a racist."

"Then you don't know me."

Mavis suddenly gets up and starts to walk away.

"I'll phone you later ..." I say weakly, a bit taken aback. She has already gone by the time I add, "And we'll talk more."

I return to the meeting. There's a loud sound of uncontrolled bawling. It is Dolores. She is upset and Jane is doing her best to console her, feeding her with an endless supply of tissues. The others look on awkwardly, though Susan also seems concerned and sits on the other side of her, gently patting her.

"I ... didn't ... mean ... to ...", Dolores whimpers incoherently.

"I'm sure Mavis is ...", Jane tries to say but Dolores interrupts. "This ... is ... just ... my ... way. When I'm nervous I'm ... loud."

52

WHO AM I?

"Perhaps we could have been more welcoming" says Jane.

"No ... no ... no," says Dolores. "You are all ... very ... welcoming."

"I'll just fetch you some tea," says Lady Thraxton, eager to do something practical to compensate for her inability to defuse the situation. Dolores looks up.

"Thank you ... you are so kind."

Lady Thraxton disappears into the kitchen. I follow her.

I can see that Lady T is slightly shaking. The teapot is in danger of spurting hot liquid everywhere and I place my hand over hers to steady her. My guess is that her living room has not been privy to such shows of emotion before and this has thrown her. I gently hold her hand, but she pulls it away. Emotions are not her thing, it seems.

"None of this is your fault, Lady Thraxton."

"My house, my responsibility ... perhaps it was a mistake bringing in two new members to such an established group."

On hearing this, I interpret her as saying, *these particular* new members. I allow her to continue as she pours out the water from the kettle.

"I can understand what Mavis has gone through," she adds.

This reinforces my suspicions of the casual racism that I detected.

"Really, Lady Thraxton? But to get up and storm out ...?"

"I think I would have done the same."

"Surely not. Look at Dolores now. You can see that she didn't mean to upset ... she just misjudged ..."

"Misjudged ... that's right. But ... dear Dawn ... would any of

WHO AM I?

'us' have misjudged ..."?

Any of us? Where did that come from?

I decide not to continue with this conversation. Instead, I leave her to it and return to the living room, where Dolores has settled down a bit. I kneel before her and speak.

"I have spoken to Mavis and ..."

I consider what to say next and decide that a white lie is in order. "She's sorry ... she has things on her mind. She'll be OK."

This seems to do the trick and Dolores smiles at me as Lady T brings in a cup of tea for her, which is gratefully received. Susan speaks up.

"In the light of these ... misunderstandings and ... the absence of Mavis ... I suggest that we close the meeting now and reconvene at our usual time next Tuesday. Is that OK ladies?"

They all nod, even Sunita, who had seemed oblivious to everything and had instead immersed herself in the book.

I wonder to myself as I grab my coat, *could this be the end of the Lovely Ladies?*

12 "So, the Lovely Ladies are, perhaps, not so ... lovely" says Derek, taking great mirth from my news.

"Just a glitch, Derek. Though ... I think our 'investigation' has been mysteriously re-routed."

"Eh? Explain?"

"We've been talking about 'identity', haven't we? You and me ... and at the book club."

"And ..." I give him a chance to put two and two together. He did, and made five!

54

WHO AM I?

"Ah, so what you're saying is that Mavis has a ... crush on the new lady, Dolores?"

"What?" I am not sure if he is joshing me as he has that grin of his that I have never been able to read properly. His grin broadens, then he speaks softly.

"Yes ... I'm not stupid, dear. Mavis has lived a sheltered life and then suddenly this larger-than-life black momma comes bounding in and she panics."

"I'm not sure if you're actually being racist here."

"Me, racist? Hey, Dawn, this is me and you. We're not racist and if we are starting to question ourselves, then ..."

"Then, what ...?"

"Then, they've won, haven't they?"

"Who have won?" I knew who he was alluding to, but I wanted to hear it anyway.

"The people Steve talked about, the manipulators ... the Marxists."

"Shall we not go there for now, Derek? Time for bed I think."

I drain my hot chocolate and race him to bed, as we are wont to do.

At breakfast time I have a phone call. It is Mavis. I am pleasantly surprised but also frustrated that perhaps it's a bit early in the day for a serious conversation, as I am sure this is going to be. I am just not too coherent before my morning coffee, so I quickly fill a cup and take it, along with the phone, into the lounge, where I curl up and make myself comfortable.

"Sorry for phoning so early, Dawn, but ... I hardly slept and I need to get this off my chest."

WHO AM I?

"Go on, Mavis. Best if you just get it out now. I may not say much, but I will be listening. Please excuse any slurping sounds." I am hoping that levity may take any sting out of whatever message she is so eager to impart at such an inconvenient time of the day.

There's a brief pause, then Mavis speaks.

"I think that this is all tied up in what we've been discussing from the book. Y'know ... identity ..."

My ears prick up. She has my full attention now, perhaps more than she realises. One thing about Mavis is that she's probably the cleverest of us all and the most perceptive. If she sees a connection as I do, then perhaps she is going to put flesh on the random thoughts I have been having. She continues.

"The more I read about ... and watch videos – there have been many of those, perhaps too many - on ... this victim culture ... with people clamouring to insist that their 'identity' is more important than all others ... the more angry I get ... and then along comes someone ..."

"Dolores?"

"Who's in one of these 'victim' groups ... of course she's probably not even aware of this ... what with the 'Black Lives Matter' and the 'giving the knee' and all the other things that are suddenly so important in our culture ... and ..."

"You felt confronted?"

"Yes ... and when it seems that she was mocking me ... I just ..."

"You couldn't handle it. So ... flight ... rather than fight."

"I'm no fighter, Dawn. I'm as meek as they come ..."

There's a silence as I gather my thoughts, clearing the early

WHO AM I?

morning cobwebs of my mind in order to say something hopefully constructive. The coffee has been helpful.

"But Mavis ... this doesn't make you racist. Instead ..."

"Yes?"

"It brings up something far more important."

Now I'm not sure where the following thoughts come from, but I sense that I am actually speaking to myself as well as Mavis. Could this be ... from somewhere outside myself? This brought back memories of the search I had already been on in our earlier adventure ... and temporarily abandoned ... for God. Has it returned? Interesting! I had been feeling very guilty of late that, despite being very worked up about the possibility of the divine, I had forsaken that particular pathway, perhaps a little too quickly. Ordinary life has that power, sometimes. Unless there is a compelling reason, we do tend to drift towards the comfort of the familiar, especially at my time of life. There are regrets, but perhaps the spark could very well be re-ignited, you never know.

"You and I are on similar paths, Mavis. Let's think about this. I told you about the 'trans' person we met, Jo-Joe, who rejected all attempts to label and classify her. And then our Susan, too. She accepts her sexuality but sees no need to celebrate it and boast about it. Now we see the same when we look at the world in general. Poor Dolores has already been judged by you – and probably others in our group – because she called herself a 'proud black woman'. I don't think she said this because she buys into all this identity thing, but rather because she has been pulled into it without even realising it."

Mavis is quiet as she takes this in, then speaks.

"How interesting. I need some time to reflect on what you've

WHO AM I?

said, Dawn. Is that OK?"

"Yes ... of course ... and what conversations we can have when we next meet up."

"Will I be welcome back?"

"Of course, Mavis. Couldn't do it without you."

We say our goodbyes and the not-so-comforting thought I have is whether Dolores herself will be back.

"I heard what you just said", comes a voice from the kitchen. Derek has been listening.

"I always knew you were the clever one ... perhaps I should tell you more often."

"Oh, don't be silly, love, now go and make me another cup of tea, this one has gone cold."

13 The next meeting of the Lovely Ladies is to be pivotal. If a cultural historian were to look back at these confusing troubled times, they would do no better than read the minutes of this particular meeting, except for the fact that no minutes were being kept. Perhaps they could interview the fly on the wall (through an interpreter of course), if indeed any of those were present too. Or, perhaps, I am being a little too melodramatic here. You judge.

Everybody was present. Lady T had wielded the party whip. *So at least she has some uses*, I think, cruelly. She starts to speak.

"Welcome back ladies. I ..."

She is interrupted by a nervous-looking Mavis, chomping at the bit to speak.

"I'm sorry, Lady Thraxton," she says, "But I just have to say something about ..."

WHO AM I?

Lady T interrupts her in turn, but in a good way, rather than in frustration through being interrupted.

"The floor is yours, Mavis." She smiles warmly at her.

Mavis begins speaking.

"I feel I have to apologise."

She turns to Dolores, who has her customary big smile, but slightly frayed at the edges.

"I was ... as I think they say ... out of order last week," says Mavis.

Dolores seems puzzled. "No, no ... I understand ... it is me who should be apologising, dearie."

They both look at each other, like two very benign prize fighters sizing each other up, pre-fight.

Jane breaks the impasse by slapping her head in mock frustration. "Oh come on, you two. Stop flapping about, kiss and make up ... and let us all get on with it!"

This brings a smile to everyone and Dolores takes the initiative and strides over to Mavis and gives her a big bear hug, almost squeezing the life out of her in the process. Mavis smiles, awkwardly, concentrating more on a continuing need to breathe! I decide to speak.

"Ladies, I've been thinking ... particularly in the light of ... recent events ... I think that our two newcomers are a ... godsend ... really."

"Interesting", says Susan. "Please go on, Dawn."

"Well ..." *I'm beginning to sound like Mavis.* "Regarding the book and our recent discussions about ... identity ... and having spoken to Mavis ..."

WHO AM I?

I glance at Mavis for permission and she gives me a faint nod and a fainter smile. I take that as consent to continue.

"We should learn from our experiences ... even our misunderstandings. Dolores ... can I speak directly to you ... can I be frank?"

"Of course ... dearie ... of course ..."

"Dawn", I remind her.

"Dawn. Yes. Be as frank as you want. This is a safe space ..."

She looks around. "Yes?" she adds, just to check with us first. We all nod and give her the affirmation she needs.

"Then here we go," I say. "Us ladies ... and I speak for at least two of us here ... have lived very ... cloistered, safe lives and ..."

"Yes dear?" Dolores has a wry smile.

"You're the first black lady that we've ever got close to ... I think?" I look around to a sea of nods. "We're a small community. Perhaps not as welcoming as we could be, so we don't get many coming from other ... you know ...". More nods. I am pretty sure that I was just saying what most are thinking here.

There's one of those awkward silences. Dolores looks a bit awkward, too.

"Really?" she says, "You need to get out more!"

Then she breaks into one of her guffaws. But I continue regardless, wondering if she's going to be laughing once I finish what I have to say.

"We've been discussing identity and the need for us to find our own ... unique identity ... rather than what society may be trying to squeeze us into ... I'm now going to be direct, Dolores ..."

60

WHO AM I?

I paused, then continue, a little hesitatingly. "What do you think about Black Lives Matter, for instance?"

Her smile briefly disappears. She is thinking.

"It's a good thing ... isn't it?" she says, slightly hesitating. "Black ... lives ... matter ... They do, don't they ladies?" Her smile returns, just slightly dimmed.

"Remember, Dawn ... safe space," says Lady T, as if I was a mischievous schoolgirl. I disregard this and carry on.

"You are among friends, Dolores, nothing I am saying is meant to be a personal attack ... this is the problem though ..."

Susan gets it and interrupts. "... we just don't talk about these things anymore," she says. "It's like ... some things are not supposed to be discussed ... and ... I have a personal stake here ... since I 'came out' a couple of weeks ago ... we haven't discussed that either."

"Came out?" says Dolores, intrigued.

"As a lesbian," adds Susan, but her tone of voice is tinged with what could be shame, which she then acknowledges. "See ... even saying the word makes me feel ... dirty ... that can't be right."

"No," I say. "Thanks, Susan for your openness."

"I for one don't think any less of you," says Lady T in a bluster, adding further awkwardness.

Suddenly an unexpected voice breaks through the silence.

"I hate Muslims."

Time freezes. The moment stretches out as we individually try and process those three words. It seems surreal, counter to the developing atmosphere of a growing understanding and

WHO AM I?

acceptance between us. And then this … *I hate Muslims.*

The voice is slight and surprisingly clear and precise, totally at odds with our perception of the hate-bearer, Sunita, the Asian lady who, up to this moment, has barely spoken a word in the two meetings she has attended. Lady T is the first to respond, in her usual bluster.

"Well I never … perhaps some things are best left unspoken."

A strange response, I feel, as if this was a sentiment shared by others, though evidently one peculiar to Lady T, thank goodness. The implication is, *of course, we all hate Muslims, we just don't talk about it.* Oh dear. I speak next.

"Did we hear you correctly, Sunita, perhaps your English … ?"

"There is nothing wrong with my 'English', Dawn. I speak perfectly good English, I have lived here for my whole life," says Sunita, with surprising confidence. She continues speaking, with clarity and conviction.

"My father was in the British Indian army and I have a British passport. I am a British Hindu, though … I prefer to be called a Hindu Briton. I am a proud British lady. How about that? I wear a sari on the outside, on the inside I am as British as any of you, even you Lady Thraxton. For your consideration, I vote Tory, love shopping at Harrods and Fortnum & Mason, read the Daily Mail and subscribe to the Spectator and Tatler."

She has certainly laid down her credentials and her chosen identity. Lady T is particularly surprised (but, I suspect, secretly delighted) and evidently lost for words. But, of course, this is just a foundation for what is to come next.

"I am judged for my colour. My father fought for this country but was just the local … 'Paki' … to those on our street, until he ran for councillor and became a pillar of the local community.

WHO AM I?

Nothing really changed, he just became *'our Paki'*, if you know what I mean. But of course, no more. It's not that people are less racist, it's just that the penalties for it are so severe. For that I have this 'woke' identity culture to thank I suppose. Been reading about it in this excellent book you have given me."

"But ... the Muslims?" I interrupt, hitting the elephant in the room straight in the face.

"Yes ... the Muslims. Of course, no love was lost between us from our country of origin, though much of the blame there falls at the feet of your ancestors, the British Empire. But I have no quarrel with the past. It's the present we must deal with ... and the future."

I thought that was very eloquently expressed, particularly from someone whom we all labelled as having a poor grasp of the English language, because of her apparent reticence. How appearances fool us! I feel chastised by this.

"So, why hate them? " asks Jane.

"Because they are trouble."

"What do you mean, 'trouble'? "

"Did you know that over three-quarters of wars in the world are initiated by Muslims ... 9/11, 7/7 in London, Islamic State, Gaza, Afghanistan, Sudan, Nigeria ...? "

We are silenced. We simply don't have the facts to contest her so remain silent. She has obviously done her research on a subject that was close to her heart, but perhaps not in a good way. There is every danger that this is going to develop into a rant and totally destroy the ambience of the meeting. Suddenly, I get a flashback to the 'call to prayer' I witnessed the other morning in our neighborhood and a flash of anger crosses my mind. I swept it away before it can grab hold of me. I feel a little

WHO AM I?

ashamed at the thought. I know that I have to do something to help the situation.

"We can't contest your facts, Sunita but … why do you … personally … hate Muslims? And is there anything we can do to help? … This is a safe place as you know."

This silences her and settles her a bit. Her tone lightens as she speaks again. This time her passion gives way to a brokenness.

"We Hindus, we just want to live in peace. We want to integrate. We respect the laws of the land … we don't want to impose … but this is not the Muslim way and … when they create mischief … we are tarred with the same brush."

"Because of the colour of your skin?" asks Susan.

"Correct. And this fuss over the Palestinians is not helping."

We all nod at this. I, of course, had been there, so I understand. But I didn't think it was right to follow that particular thread. She continues.

"Islamophobia … have you thought about it? A phobia is an 'irrational' fear, yet a fear of Muslims is so very … rational … because of what I just told you. Where is the Hinduphobia? Where is our protection, eh? Do we have to be violent in order to get noticed?"

This is greeted by silence. She relaxes.

"There, I've said my piece. Got it off my chest now … I'm sorry, but I do actually … feel better for it … and for that, I must thank you all." She leans back into her seat, picks up her book and begins reading, now seemingly embarrassed over her outburst and deflecting. We try not to notice. Lady T is not quite so subtle in her response.

"Glad to be of service" she says through gritted teeth, clearly

WHO AM I?

angry that her pleasant little gathering has been seemingly hijacked by sectarian politics. Mavis speaks next.

"Thank you, Sunita, for your ... honesty. Wow, what a mixed ... and mixed-up ... bunch we are here."

At that, we all laugh, even Lady T, who usually seems to be one step behind the rest of us. Mavis continues.

"But Muslims ... you talk about tarring with the same brush ... but you're in danger of tarring all Muslims with the same brush. I know quite a few Muslims and they are most civilised and peacekeeping."

"I agree," I say. "Derek's dentist is Muslim and you couldn't meet a nicer man. You wouldn't want someone you didn't trust to be fiddling inside your mouth with sharp objects, would you?"

That draws a few chuckles.

"My doctor is a Muslim too," says Susan. "And a lovely chap to boot."

Sunita nods her head and looks up briefly, before returning to her reading. You can see that she has conceded the point. She looks up again and speaks.

"Yes of course," she says. "I too have a decent relationship with my Muslim neighbour ... nevertheless ..."

"OK," I interrupt. "But what does this ... teach us ... and how can we help Sunita?"

A voice pipes up, one that we haven't heard for some time. It is Dolores.

"Actually, ladies ... Black Lives Matter? You were asking me."

That now seems like an age ago, now. This is turning out to be

WHO AM I?

a very eventful meeting. Hopefully, it will be remembered for all of the right reasons. I am determined to do my bit to ensure it will be.

And then I have one of my special 'moments', as when I was speaking to Dawn over the phone yesterday. Or so I thought.

"There is a connection here … between Sunita and her concerns and Dolores … though we don't yet know your concerns. Again, it is 'identity' that ties it all together, I think. Sunita, you are no different to Susan here and Jo-Joe, my 'trans' acquaintance, in that you want to be free to live your life simply as 'you', not through reference to your gender or race. Am I right?"

They both nod in agreement.

"And you, Dolores. The same, I think. Perhaps you feel you have to project a version of yourself that is approved by others, but may not be … you. Although we haven't talked about Black Lives Matter and all that surrounds it, but … I get the feeling that you would prefer just to be known as … Dolores, rather than 'black' Dolores. Am I right?"

She thinks for a bit, then answers me.

"No … I don't think you are, Dawn … Sorry."

14 I gave Derek the full run-down on my return home. He is astonished that a group of unassuming ladies could generate 'such drama'. My pride takes a bit of a battering, though, in my faulty reading of Dolores and what drives her. This niggles me a lot, but I won't let it overwhelm me. I'm exhausted by the whole thing and wonder whether I'm in too deep, or, even worse, totally out of my depth. Derek reassures me that this is not so and reminds me what we learned from our previous adventure, *follow the evidence, then act on it*. Perhaps there is more evidence to come before conclusions

WHO AM I?

can be made? This thought proved correct, as subsequent events unfolded.

Today we have a day out planned to London. We intend to visit the new Museum of London in Docklands, a place that we've meant to go to for a long time, but never quite managed. We aimed to get there for the opening at 10am, which would give us plenty of scope for planning the rest of the day. I am particularly interested in the reconstructions of life as it was a century or so ago when the docks were a going concern, as my grandfather was a London docker for most of his life and I am intrigued to know whether the tales he spun about his everyday life actually matched with reality.

We arrive and are told that, for the 'full experience' we should start at the third floor and work our way down. We reluctantly agreed, though the installation there, *London, sugar & slavery,* did not hold much interest for either of us. Conscious of our step timers, with our gruelling 10,000 a day targets, we opted for the stairs and arrived at the top floor puffing and panting, to be greeted by a wall display charting ships and their captains and start and end points of journeys … and the number of 'enslaved Africans' (they refuse to use the word 'slaves') carried, usually between 200 and 300 of the poor souls. All are presented in such a matter-of-fact manner, but incredible to think that barely two hundred years ago it was acceptable to treat fellow human beings so. Of course, it still happens, human trafficking is a huge enterprise, but it is now an *illegal* enterprise, certainly not state-sponsored. Food for thought, certainly.

The next display called this *one of the great crimes against humanity.* Yet by the 1780s about 15,000 ex-slaves were living freely in London, some of them having done quite well for themselves, despite other Africans still being transported at that time to the

WHO AM I?

West Indies. The exhibition focussed on the sugar plantations in the Caribbean and we read that the original slaves were the white, political prisoners from the British Isles until the 1680s, when the African slave trade started, presumably because it was cheaper, regarding the workers just as commodities. That was, of course, the sordid underbelly of the British Empire, the constant drive for a profit at the expense of others.

It was interesting reading comments scrawled on a card display, presumably by schoolkids. 'What was happening a long time ago was so horrible. I can't believe it was normal.' 'To see humans do that to one another is something very sad and heartbreaking.' 'I am both overwhelmed and empowered. As a descendant of some of the kidnapped and trafficked human beings, I am proud to be here to represent their legacy, I am their wildest dreams!'

The displays had clearly struck a chord with the younger generation and I thought that commendable, as we are so used to hearing negative stories about these future citizens.

"That last one is particularly poignant," I remark.

"Yes, it is. We humans are amazingly resilient. These descendants have thrived and put their past behind them. That's good to see."

"Yes, it is. There's hope for us all yet, eh? At last some positivity, it's good to hear."

"Yes," he replies, a pensive expression on his face. It was then that I suddenly felt so good about the way Derek and I had found a common cause, working as a team. It turns out that we actually made a pretty good team and I found this ... nice ... for want of a more eloquent expression. I smile at him and he smiles back, a little quizzically, as if he couldn't quite read me.

WHO AM I?

Well, that's a typical man for you. Still can't figure me out after decades of living together. I chuckle and he chuckles back, hedging his bets.

I nod and start thinking about Dolores. Has she put this past behind her, assuming that her ancestors were caught up in this evil enterprise? Or am I overthinking? Probably.

Another panel is quite thought-provoking, asserting that London has grown rich based on the slave trade and that 'Africa beats in the heart of our city'. I made a mental note to check that out, as I felt that this statement was a little too ... I wasn't sure of the word ... it just didn't ring true for me. These days I have grown into the realisation that I really need to check everything, though it's not always obvious how to do so. Nevertheless, the truth is a treasured commodity and we must serve it at all times. *Now where did that thought come from?*

The final section is the most intriguing and, I must confess, I have never seen its ilk in any other museum or exhibition before. It is introduced by the panel, 'how are you feeling?', with the theme of 'reclaiming emotions'. Attention has suddenly switched from the story of the slaves to us, the visitors and the effect all of this has on us. Very unusual for an exhibition to do this, I thought.

Although this exhibition dates back to 2007, this section has only recently been added, as a collaboration between two mental health charities as a result of 'young people spending days learning, exploring emotions and processing them, using mindfulness techniques'. It is a powerful display, including objects from Africa that you can smell to conjure up healing thoughts and a film of testimonies from young people. You are then given somewhere to sit, reflect and process your emotions and write them on cards, for display. There's a visual aid to help

WHO AM I?

you, a circle divided into segments, covering such emotional responses as 'fearful', 'angry', 'sad', 'happy', 'surprised' and 'low'. These, too, are subdivided. For instance, the 'happy' category, which, at first, seemed a bit out of place here, had subdivisions of 'interested', 'proud', 'curious', 'valued', 'sensitive' and 'hopeful'. This evidently covers the emotional response linked to the emancipation process, of the collapse of the slave system, thanks to reformers like William Wilberforce. There are even leaflets you can take home with you, for further study, though there are none left at the moment.

"How do you feel about this?" I ask Derek.

"Feeling ... about feelings ..." he says enigmatically.

I nod, knowingly. He always had a way with words, my husband.

Although we say no more about this, I can see some cogs whirring in Derek's head as we sit sipping our fruit teas in the museum café. I leave him to his thoughts as I pop over to the ladies' toilets, which, I must say, are one of the very best I have encountered in a museum. I respond accordingly by granting a five-star review with one of those wall-mounted response gadgets. I return to a pensive husband.

"What's up, Derek?" I ask. "There's something going on in that bonce of yours."

"Yes there is," he says, finally. "It is early still, Dawn ... are you up for something different?"

I am intrigued. I can see zeal in his eyes and I don't want to extinguish it, so I say, "I am putty in your hands, master. Lead me on ..."

And he does. We walk down to Westferry DLT station, take a train to Bank station and then hop on the intriguing Waterloo

WHO AM I?

to Bank train, surely a curiosity from the past, linking just two stations, with no stops in-between, in an indecently swift journey. From Waterloo we walk, notching up more welcome steps for our phone apps, arriving at the Imperial War Museum in Lambeth. *How intriguing. I wonder what the connection is?*

The second floor is his destination. My heart skips, but not in a nice way, when I see that it is the Holocaust Galleries that he has taken me to. I freeze at the entrance.

"Really?" I say.

"Yes … but not for a detailed study, just a quick whistle-stop tour."

"Really?" I repeat.

"Yes, really. I am intrigued to see whether the creators have added a 'how are you feeling' section?"

"I see where you're going on this but … can't we just ask one of the guides here?"

"Remember our promise to ourselves, Dawn … follow the evidence … I wouldn't take anyone's word for it, we need to discover things for ourselves."

"Right … but …"

I had no words and I let him lead me onwards. He clearly felt very strongly about this. I had fewer words as we rushed through it with our best approximation of tunnel-vision, trying not to be drawn into the growing ever-depressing story. The stories displayed were compelling, but emotion-sapping as the story unfolded of how a civilised industrialised nation can use their hatred and technology to wipe out over six million lives in the most horrific manner. Only one exhibit really stopped me in my tracks, though. I just had to stop for reflection. Derek too.

WHO AM I?

The shoes. Thousands of them, collected from Jewish children arriving at the Auschwitz death camp. All in a pile, in public view. No words. It is impossible not to be moved by this, whatever your background or inclination. Just by being a functional human being ensures that your emotions are stirred up. There is no escape. There was no escape for Derek and I and we were sobbing quite openly, something that I don't think I had seen from Derek since our honeymoon (and I won't say any more about that.)

"How are you feeling?" asks Derek as we leave the exhibition.

"Exhausted," I answer.

"Me too ... but how do we process this? The exhibition just finishes, leaves us in an emotional state and then says 'goodbye', as if what we've just seen is just ... ordinary."

"Yes ... unlike the Sugar and Slavery exhibition."

"Quite ... but which one has left us the most emotionally drained?"

"Interesting observation, Derek ... perhaps we should discuss this? "

"I think we need help."

I knew exactly what he meant by this.

15 So here we are, yet again sitting in a café waiting for 'Podcast Steve' to turn up. So much had happened since we last met him, that I barely knew where to start but our recent experiences at the museums were fresh in our minds and so we decided to start there. When Steve turns up, with his customary coffee already bought, Derek hits him with all barrels, as soon as the niceties are over.

"Steve, are people still moved by the Holocaust?"

WHO AM I?

Steve is startled. He doesn't see that one coming.

"That's some question, where on earth has that come from, Derek?"

"We went to the Holocaust exhibition at the Imperial War Museum yesterday."

"Ah yes … very poignant. Try to go back now and again when I can."

"Why?" I ask.

"Just to remember … many would rather forget."

There's a danger that our conversation would divert away from our current journey, so I decide to be more specific and expand the conversation to take in the first part of our day.

"We also went to the Sugar and Slavery exhibition at the London Museum and thought that we'd contrast the two."

"Really?" he exclaims. "Surely a big difference."

"What do you mean?"

"Assuming the first is about the West Indies slave trade, that one is an injustice from a few centuries ago that was brought to an end through legislation … the other is a culmination of centuries of hatred which … as you already know … has no sign of ending."

"Yes, we know that," says Derek, perhaps a little too brusquely. "But …"

Steve is interested, but I could see his hackles were up. Derek continues.

"The Slavery exhibition had a final station where you can examine and process your emotions after what you've seen, but the Holocaust exhibition had nothing. As you leave the exhibition, you are just led to the stairs and then the exit. It's all so … I don't know …"

"… we're just trying to process that, Steve," I interrupt.

He is thoughtful and careful with his words. He can sense our heightened emotions.

"Yes … I can see the contrast now. I don't think there's anything sinister going on here. The Holocaust exhibition, I imagine, was created and funded by the Jewish community. Their aim was to provide the facts, to counter all the falsehoods and … attempted revisionism."

"Revisionism?"

"Yes … some still deny it actually happened."

"My goodness," I gasped. "I never knew … how awful."

"Yes, I could say more on that but, I think, that's not a journey for now."

"I agree," adds Derek. "So, what about the Slavery exhibition?"

"This has a very different objective I would think. I suspect that the 'examine your emotions' part of it is a charity initiative."

"Yes, it is. Two charities … 'Mind' and 'Taking Shape Association'."

"Mind is well-known, very much in the 'woke universe' and has been around for a bit. Not heard of the other one."

"OK," I say. "So, what you're thinking is that 'examine your emotions' is very much in line with the 'current agenda' we've been talking about."

"Yes," he replies, "whenever 'feelings' are emphasised you can be assured that there will be a 'woke' initiative behind it."

There's a silence, so he continues.

WHO AM I ?

"What you have observed can be looked at in two ways. First in terms of mindsets. The Jewish mindset that created the Holocaust exhibition is to emphasis education and understanding primarily, whereas the 'woke' mindset behind the Slavery display is to emphasise emotional response, to encourage us to be 'affected' in some way ..."

"And shouldn't we?" I ask. "Be affected?"

"Yes, of course we should. But ... shouldn't that be in a way that is right for you, rather than imposing it, or expecting it. You can't fail but be affected by the Holocaust exhibition but we will all process it in different ways I think ... I just think that is different from encouraging us to be emotionally engaged as a shared experience ... fitting us into a mould of expectations ... or ... is that just me being cynical?"

"Will have to get back to you on that one, Steve," I say. Derek is more thoughtful.

"Are you implying manipulation, Steve?"

"I suppose I am, Derek, but that's how I see it. The world is full of it."

Our silence gives him the licence to continue.

"Everywhere you look we are encouraged to see the world through our emotions. That's why so many are cancelled ... with the intention 'let's keep them away from us just in case they anger or upset us.' We are encouraged to judge people through the emotions they stir up in us, rather than what they are objectively saying. If they are somehow allowed to give opinions or perform to an audience they're drowned out by the mob."

"Why is this so? Can you expand on this?"

WHO AM I?

"Apparently, we are so sensitive these days that there are a whole load of words we can't use, or attitudes we can't have, just in case it offends someone. An extreme case are those councils who have banned the use of the word 'Christmas' in case it offends Muslims or others. The fact is that no-one is actually offended, but the restrictions are put in place anyway … just in case!"

"Who makes up these rules, Steve?"

"Good question, Dawn. Who does the cancelling anyway? Who are the thought police these days? Who knows?"

He throws his hands up in the air in mock despair. He continues.

"There's a whole load of words we can't use any more, words that were freely bandied about just a few years ago … I think I'd better stop now."

"I get your point but can it not be that they actually do care for us … in some sort of weird way?"

"Really? Just like those with banners of support for Palestinians really care for them? If they really cared for them they would be calling for Hamas to stop hiding behind them."

"Yes we heard that one before."

"There's enough crocodile tears at these demos, whatever they are complaining about, to fill a swamp … full of crocodiles!"

We feel he's just made that one up, as it didn't quite scan, but he's on a roll.

"How many times have you watched Dad's Army, or 'til Death us do Part, or even Fawlty Towers on one of those nostalgia stations, only to get a trigger warning, to warn us that we may be offended? Apparently 'Terry and June' has discriminatory

WHO AM I?

language and 'Hi-de-Hi!' has the 'language and attitudes of an era that may offend us now' … offend us now? … have we turned into quivering babies in just a couple of decades …? "

"OK. OK." Derek has had enough. "You've made your point."

"Just one more," adds Steve, calming down a little.

"All this … It's called virtue signalling."

"I've heard of that," I say, "but never quite understood what it is."

"It's when people pretend that they care, so that they are considered 'good sorts' by our culture. The worst offenders are the corporates, the supermarkets, hotel chains and retailers, with their Pride Months and their LGBT-friendly slogans. It's nothing about caring, but all about the loss of profit if they are seen not to care!"

After a silence he adds, "Rant over … I'm starting to get on my own nerves now … this just makes it so easy to be cynical."

I nod in agreement and change the subject.

"Understood … Steve, you mentioned earlier that there were two ways of looking at the exhibitions we went to. You only gave us the first."

"Yes … yes, Dawn. Well remembered … trouble is that to answer you, I'm going to have to be … cynical … again … You asked about the differences in approach between the two, one that catered for the feelings of the visitors and the other that didn't. The fact is that these days, the black population are high up in the 'victim hierarchy' … you only have to look at George Floyd and the 'taking of the knee' by our footballers to see that … but Jews? Nowhere to be seen. No one really cares. Black history month and Pride weeks are thrust upon us, but if you

WHO AM I?

knew the brouhaha surrounding the keeping of the Holocaust Remembrance Day, then you'll realise that Jews are not to be found anywhere in this 'victim hierarchy'.

"So sad," adds Derek. "I tell you what, let's have a break. I'll get some more coffees, that OK?"

We nod and he disappears. I use this window to bring up what's really on my mind, our two new Lovely Ladies. I give him a quick precis of the tensions uncovered at the last meeting. He is thoughtful as he considers.

"The Asian lady ..."

"Sunita."

"... Sunita. It's hard to take issue with her. As they say, we need to walk in each other's boots to appreciate what they go through. If you've spent your whole life trying your best to conform, but again and again being judged by such a random thing as skin pigmentation ... there's nothing worse to see others in the same boat as yourself behaving badly and just giving ammunition to the haters."

"I just don't understand how racism works," I confess. "Perhaps it's the way I've been brought up, but I just don't see skin colour, just the person. I've had scores of friends of all colours ... but they are all just friends, people. If I'm going to judge someone, it's for their behaviour, not their appearance."

"I have to say it's the same for me," says Derek, who has just returned and caught the gist of the conversation. "Are we unusual?"

"Perhaps you are," says Steve. "Especially in your generation, our generation – the baby boomers. You had grown up in a culture that had a growing resentment against Blacks and Asians ... it was just how things were then. I'm of the same

WHO AM I?

generation and it's the same for me too."

"Then that must make us the good guys," says Derek. "The Tolerant Three ... superheroes."

We laugh.

"Dolores." I bring up the name now. I had been putting this one off. Her response to me still has me bamboozled.

"She's a proud black lady," Steve says. "Is there really anything wrong with that? Is there anything wrong in feeling good about yourself?"

"No, of course not."

"Then admit to her that you have misread her ... and apologise. That's all you can do."

We say our goodbyes and Steve gives me a draft of his forthcoming book, "A Matter of Identity", which he suggests will help us in our current adventure. I put it aside to read later, perhaps much later.

16 It's as if the *Lovely Ladies Literary Loungers* had morphed into something new, something more than just a parochial village book club for ladies of leisure. The last couple of meetings had taken a lot out of me, not a person at home with tension and controversy. I was even beginning to fear the next meeting and even wondering if there would be a next meeting for me. But salvation is provided for me in the way of a chance meeting with Dolores in the car park of the local Tesco.

Thankfully she sees me first. If it had been the other way round, I'm sure I would have hidden behind a trolley booth or bent down to tie up non-existent laces. First contact comes with one of her trademark bear-hugs, wrapping me like a tight-fitting

WHO AM I?

pullover, arms trapped and totally at her mercy.

"Dawn ... how wonderful to see you. What a surprise. I saw you as a Waitrose person ... surely you aren't slumming it here?"

The guffaws come freely and I laugh too. "I'm poorer than I look, Dolores. Just a boring old pensioner really."

"Or a proud white woman ... eh?"

She has a wicked glint in her eye. And with that remark, all tension begins to dissipate. The proud elephant in the room has been addressed. It's as if she had said, *no harm done, Dawn. No harm done.*

"Are we OK?" I ask.

"Of course. There's always going to be awkwardness between people who don't really know each other, eh?"

"Yes ... but I was wrong to jump in and speak up for you ... I was a bit full of myself then, I think."

"Yes, I think you were." *Do I hear a hint of seriousness here? Have I touched a nerve? Awkward!*

"And for that ... I apologise."

"Apology accepted." *Aha, so there was something to apologise for.*

"What you have to understand, Dawn, is that being a proud black woman is something we have had to fight for, growing up in a white world."

I can only nod at this as this is her experience, not mine. As with Sunita, I haven't walked in her shoes. She continues.

"The world has changed, Dawn ... somehow we have finally been accepted in society. Most of the fighting is done ... finished. No-one uses the 'N' word anymore, yet I heard it all the time growing up in Harlesden ... that has to be a good

WHO AM I?

thing, eh?"

"Oh yes ... changing times."

"And if footballers want to 'give the knee' then let them ..."

There's a second of awkwardness here that I'm sure she notices. I am tempted to interrupt her flow but, weighing things up, I think that misunderstandings would be very likely. I let things stand and change the subject.

"Coming next Tuesday?"

She considers her reply. "Don't think so, Dawn. Not really my people ... though you're OK."

At that she hugs me again and I suspect this is her way of saying goodbye as she takes her trolley and disappears into the supermarket.

I can't tell you how disappointed I am. Have we inadvertently 'cancelled' her? It seems like a failure on my part. Perhaps the days are numbered for the Lovely Ladies? All sorts of scenarios run through my mind as that chance encounter is re-run. In every one I win her over with clever rhetoric and sincerity. But, alas, we don't get re-runs, otherwise there would be few mistakes made in our world and, let's face it, much of our world runs on mistakes and misunderstandings. That's what being human is all about, isn't it?

Our bedtime ritual is tinged with sadness for me. Derek picks up on this.

"There's nothing you did wrong, love," he says.

"But there must have been something I could have said. When she said that she wasn't coming any more there must have been something I could have said to ... y'know ... make her reconsider."

WHO AM I?

"If you had to live through that again, would it be any different? " he asks.

"Not really, though, goodness knows, I've run this through again and again in my mind. I'm exhausted! It probably wouldn't have been any different, whatever I would have said … I think her mind was already made up."

"Then you have a clear conscience."

"Perhaps," I concede. "But it's still a failure."

"But not yours, dear, you did your best. It's all a part of this crazy divided world they have created for us … our masters!"

"Suppose so."

Derek attempts to lighten things up. "Never mind … remember, we're visiting the 'Twilight Zone' tomorrow. That will cheer you up." He is being ironic.

17 Ash Tree Heights care home had seen better days. But it had also seen worse days, apparently, before the government had bunged them a bit more cash. This had been the result of some mysterious goings-on there weeks earlier, that is only now filtering through to the public domain (and will be recorded in a new book soon to be published by this same author).

Derek's father, Sidney, is a resident there. Now 98 years old with advanced dementia and Alzheimer's, visits are quite problematic. Yet the place is full of life, thanks to the manageress, Deidrie, and her staff. It is a place of stories and surprises, which is why we call it 'the Twilight Zone'. You never know what's going to happen there next.

We are greeted by Ruby, the assistant manager, when we arrive. A pleasant, neat lady, dressed elegantly in a matching skirt and

WHO AM I?

blouse, she is always kind and courteous and leads us to the secure unit, which is Sidney's new home. He had been in a less-supervised section on the first floor but had been proven to be a bit of a 'problematic guest'. He had acquired an 'arch-enemy', another elderly resident, but a rather nasty one and punch-ups were rather too regular for the staff's tastes. These were mostly instigated by Sidney's nighttime wanderings through the corridor, his brain clouded by dementia and his sense of direction totally kaput. Often this led him into other residents' rooms (the doors were never locked), including his adversary, who took great exception at being woken up at 3am and mistaken for Sidney's long-since-departed wife, Derek's mother.

He is in the lounge, sitting up in a chair and fast asleep. Around him are six ladies and a man, all in various states of mental confusion and physical ineptitude. We draw up a couple of chairs on either side of him and whisper to him so that he wakes up gently and without trauma. I stroke his arm tenderly. He opens his eyes and smiles. There is some recognition of Derek and perhaps of me, too.

"Dad," whispers Derek. "How've you been?"

His dad smiles but says nothing. Derek reaches into his pocket and fetches an open packet of jelly babies, his dad's favourite food. Apparently, diabetes and high cholesterol have been defeated somehow by his unique metabolism. Only cornflakes and bacon can compete in his limited culinary universe. Derek feeds the jelly babies into his father's toothless mouth as we both attempt to make conversation. He gradually gains awareness and suddenly blurts out 'my little boy' as he fully recognises his son. We are always amused at this familiarity.

He only really perks up when I show him family photos on my iPhone, particularly the babies and toddlers in the family, which

WHO AM I?

elucidate the same response 'andsome. So 'andsome. All this has become a weekly ritual. For the hour or so we are there, there is a tentative connection but, outside that precious time window his father has no recollection of the visit or any before. In fact, his memory fails him literally minutes after our visit. What a way to live. The only saving grace is the knowledge that he is well looked after here, fed, clothed and cleaned up after his 'little accidents', too gruesome to relate here. Those carers deserve medals!

We would both guiltily admit that the only real pleasure we get on these occasions is when we visit the main lounge, where we find the residents who are a bit more 'compos mentis' gathered around the perimeter, under the auspices of the gangly ever-cheerful Lee, the part-time entertainments manager, himself older than many of the residents, but with still a 'lot of lead in his pencil'.

We are greeted with a lot of affection by those who remember our faces. We help out by talking with them and perhaps running a quiz or playing some music from yesterday (the 1960s a particular favourite – many here, incredibly, are ex-hippies) through a blue-tooth speaker. The residents love it and so do we. The reason why I have brought this all up is that this half-hour is like an excursion into our shared past, a far different place to where we are now and a welcome dip into a time when things were so less complicated.

It's like being taken back in time to the days of *On the Buses* or *'Allo 'Allo,* with the bawdy humour, casual innuendos, fruity language and disdain of the woke issues that exercise the current generation. One great big subversive bubble, outside the jurisdiction of the 'thought police'. It is one big safe space and it's not just the residents that occupy it but many of the carers

WHO AM I?

too, who have no truck with political correctness and modern attitudes, but just want to feel free to be themselves. Deidre has surely built up a safe haven here. A 'cheerful cockney', she is definitely old-school and somehow manages to run the place free of the burdensome rules and regulations that usually plague care homes these days. The events of a few weeks back, mentioned earlier but not explained, surely have a lot to do with it and I, for one, can't wait for the book that will tell all!

Derek and I love this and this is why we come. It's as therapeutic for us as it is for the residents here. It's strange but we expect that we'll continue visiting this place long after Sidney has gone to a better place (hopefully).

Here is a group of people, residents and carers alike, who are secure in their identity, even if dementia may be eating away at it on the margins. They are who they are. There are people here from a whole variety of racial backgrounds and even if one or two may have gay tendencies or any other differences, to be honest, it runs secondary to their persona and their place in the community. Lee has started up a game of family fortunes, with some obscure scenarios thought up in that strange brain of his. "We asked a hundred people, what flavour doughnut they prefer …". Hands shoot up. Perhaps they think that a clever answer would actually earn them a doughnut. It hardly matters, as the main thing is that they're all having fun. Old age and/or mental confusion certainly has its advantages. No marches or demonstrations for them, just the promise of an imaginary doughnut.

Perhaps this is the only normal place there is any more? Now, there's a thought.

WHO AM I?

18 The next morning, I had an intriguing call from 'Podcast Steve'. I was surprised to hear his voice, to be honest, because, for such a busy man, he had spent an awful lot of time with boring old Derek and me. He was quite excited. His fellow podcaster, Dave, is travelling down to London to take in a show, but also to join a rally in Trafalgar Square and he would like us to accompany him. *How wonderful,* I thought. *I wonder where this was going to take us?*

'Podcast Dave' is tall, smartly dressed with a playful scouse accent. He is also a self-confessed nerd and 'cheese merchant'. The show that he had just seen was the 'Abba Voyage' extravaganza, the digital virtual reality live show. He was buzzing. Apparently being crammed in with thousands of screaming housewives and 'fabulous' people for a couple of hours, listening to pop tunes delivered by holograms, is right up his alley. He is a complex character, especially when we get to know him better. He has a better grip and understanding of our culture and politics than anyone we have met so far and so is the perfect person to accompany us to what is promised to be 'the biggest patriotic rally the UK has ever seen.'

It is going to be an interesting day as, first, he is going to take us to a counter-demo, in Russell Square, arranged by Jeremy Corbyn and his cohorts, to show their displeasure at the fact that the "far right" is being allowed to gather in Trafalgar Square. We have encountered these people before, more so Derek, so we weren't exactly looking forward to this. But, as 'Podcast Dave' tells us, it will allow us to form a complete picture of the cultural landscape. Amazingly there is to be a third demo, a *Trans Pride* event, 'Pride in London', calling for 'justice and liberation' for all. We knew what that meant and felt that we'd seen enough Palestinian flags to last a lifetime, so we promised ourselves to give that one a wide berth.

WHO AM I?

We arrive at Russell Square at 11am, a full hour before their march to Whitehall. The Marxists, who were running the show, already had their stalls out, literally. Derek tells me that they are the same stalls he saw laid out at the pro-Palestinian demo all those weeks ago. It was the same people at the heart of both demos, which is interesting in itself and very telling. The 'Socialist Workers Party' supplied most of the banners to be brandished with slogans such as *Trans Rights now, Freedom for Palestine, Smash Fascism & Racism* and *Refugees welcome*. 'Stand up to Racism' sported posters saying *No to Racism, No to Fascism* and *Oppose Islamophobia*. 'Stop the War coalition' focussed entirely on their hatred of Israel, as did 'Counterfire', with tee shirts proclaiming 'Free Palestine' (with a map of Israel, 'totally reclaimed') and a fierce Palestinian-looking warrior proclaiming 'Revolution'!

Every slogan is a protest. Antisemitism is, as usual, the key driver to most of them. Hatred is the intended emotion, directed towards Israel and Tommy Robinson, the 'apparently fascist' organiser of the Trafalgar Square rally. There is also a stand, manned by Middle Eastern men, selling wrist bands and badges, all with a Palestinian theme.

After a few minutes of this, we retire to a park bench in the Square.

"Thoughts?" suggests Dave.

"For a counter demo against ... well, we don't really know yet ... the Palestine theme is central yet again," says Derek. "I still can't get my head around this."

"Yes, it is startling," agrees Dave. "For a group that promotes peace and justice ... they are incredibly blinkered and selective ... Muslims are killing Muslims and Christians all over the world, yet not a sausage. The focus, as ever, is on Israel, it's the

WHO AM I?

only cause that riles them up, which is a good indicator as to the state of their minds."

"Yes, Dawn and I have been there, Dave. We learned a lot from your friend, Steve."

"Good, then we don't need to dwell on it. As important as it is, it will be just a distraction."

I am, quite unusually, speechless, trying to gather my thoughts. Apart from the grizzled veteran socialists here, I am seeing very few Muslims, despite the Palestine theme and am dismayed to see so many young people, some of them young, probably still at school. I remember, early on in the Gaza conflict, how many schools were given permission for their children to go off on anti-Israel marches on some Fridays. How awful and misguided. I grieve for these people here. Why have they bought into such hatred, can't they see better paths for themselves? I get a flash of anger against those who have led them into this blind alley of negativity.

Why does this all seem about protestation, rather than celebration? This seems to be a movement that attracts people who must be very dissatisfied with their lives and grab onto this as some kind of outlet. I'm no psychologist, but this is what my instinct tells me. So sad.

We've had enough and start walking towards the Strand, where the other march is to begin. We pass by a group of noisy brutish-looking men outside a pub, many adorned with union jacks. My heart sinks. Maybe the Russell Square people are right, we are going to join a march of drunken football right-wingers? I glance at Derek and I can see he is having the same thought. We press on. Suddenly the crowd thickens and we turn a corner.

We are greeted with an incredible sight. Thousands upon

WHO AM I ?

thousands of people of all ages and varieties. Men, women and children, family groups, white people and people of colour, all mixed up and united. Union jacks, English, Welsh and Scottish flags. Flags of other nations, even Israel (but no Palestinian flags). No banners or hateful slogans, just unbridled patriotism. And joy and togetherness. Strangers are talking to each other, exchanging stories, or just gawping in amazement at the atmosphere. A few slogans are sung, one or two perhaps a little unsavoury. But also *Land of Hope and Glory* and *Rule Britannia*. It was just like a Royal occasion, but it wasn't a Royal occasion. It was a patriotic crowd that didn't need the excuse of the House of Windsor at its heart, though Royal images abounded.

I turn to Dave. He is weeping. He notices me and I look away to spare his embarrassment. I start crying too, my emotions locking into the atmosphere. I think of the labels that the counter-demo has attached to this rally, a 'gathering of fascists and racists' and the penny drops. The only fascism and racism we have seen was at Russell Square and, by now, is being displayed on the streets of London as they march down to Whitehall, venting their spleens.

Our march starts, now that the organisers have arrived, including Tommy Robinson, surrounded by a phalanx of beefy bodyguards. He is clearly a massive hero to these people, his name declared as if a football chant. At the front of the march are a group of Christians, dressed in red and white, displaying a gospel banner and 'Jesus is King' flags. A preacher shouts his message through a loud hailer. It is splendidly chaotic, a disorganised expression of joy and intent.

We arrive at Trafalgar Square in bright sunshine. Admiral Nelson tips us a wink from his lofty position. Very soon the place is packed solid, perhaps 40,000+ people here. The police

WHO AM I?

are in evidence but parked as observers on the boundaries, as there is no anti-social behaviour. A stage has been set up from which we hear speeches from a variety of speakers, including war veterans. There is also music from a gospel group and invited guests add their thoughts to the developing story. The atmosphere is both electric and heart-warming. *If this is a fascist gathering of racists then I'm a monkey's uncle!* We stay for about an hour and then walk down to the Embankment, passing a whole squadron of unused police squad wagons. We sit together on a park bench overlooking the river.

"I'm thinking," says Dave. "The rally happening now in Hyde Park, the trans demo, call themselves, 'Pride in London'. What a nonsense. We have just seen real pride in action. People united and proud of their inheritance, of their identity ..."

"... Identity," I interrupt. "This is it, isn't it? "

"Eh? " responds Derek.

"Don't interrupt", I bark at him. "Hear me out ... for the last few weeks we've been looking at 'identity' haven't we, Derek? "

"Yes," he says, still unsure as to where this is going. I continue.

"That's surely what we've seen here."

"Yes, I think I get you," says Dave, smiling like a beneficent uncle.

"Then carry on ... you'll explain it better," I suggest. He does.

"For too long now, ordinary people in this country have been ignored, marginalised. Politicians and the media have neglected them ... Why? ... Because the establishment has their own narrative to follow ..."

"Narrative? " says Derek.

"Yes ... their own version of how they want the country to

WHO AM I?

change and adapt ..."

"Adapt to what?"

"That's the thing ... no-one really knows, yet they have this ... instinct ... that we must follow a new path ... whatever that may be?"

"Sounds like the blind leading the blind."

"But it isn't because ... some of us are NOT blind ... the silent majority showed them that at Brexit ... they totally underestimated the will of the people ... the sort of people we have just seen in Trafalgar Square. The heart of England."

"Also Scotland, Wales and Northern Ireland," I suggest.

"Of course."

"Ordinary people."

"Right ... and I tell you something else ... those in charge of our country will be looking at what we've seen happening today ... and they will be shocked."

"Shocked? Why?"

"Because it doesn't fit this ... new narrative. Tommy Robinson and his friends ... are meant to be fascists and racists ... it was not meant to turn out like this. So many people here ... how can they ignore it this time?"

I decide to interrupt. "... before you continue, can you tell me something ... who exactly is this Tommy Robinson and why do they hate him so much?"

"Yes ... good question ... Tommy Robinson."

He pauses to gather his thoughts then continues.

"It depends who you ask ... you saw the crowd's reaction to him earlier ... he's the one person they think is standing up to the Islamic excesses that are being allowed to creep in ... and they love him for this ... but therein lies the reason the establishment hate him ... because of his focus on Islamic incursions, he is considered an Islamophobe and a racist and a fascist and a nazi and every other name tag they wish to throw at him ..."

"But," says Derek, "I know enough about him to know he has a chequered past."

"Oh yes ... BNP, BNP, EDL ... there's a long list of them here ... he's been involved in a lot of very unsavoury and definitely racist organisations."

"So is the Tommy Robinson of today the same Tommy Robinson who was doing that racist stuff then?"

"They say a leopard doesn't change his spots."

"But what if he has ...?"

"He's certainly filed down his rough edges and broadened his appeal so that even you and I are discussing him without feeling ... dirty ... still needs a bit more media training in my opinion. For me ... I'm still undecided ..."

"And if it needs someone like him to highlight things that, perhaps, are not right ... as he seems to be doing ... ?"

"Churchill wasn't the nicest person ... but he got us through the war", Derek suggests.

"Then let's say the jury is out over our Tommy. Let us wait and see ... judge by his fruits."

Dave then continues. "Now, back to the rally ... in terms of the negative reaction to it from the 'establishment' ... are we saying that displaying union jacks and singing patriotic songs are now meant to be some sort of 'harking back to our colonial past' ...

WHO AM I?

and we all know where these particular ideas are coming from don't we?"

He pauses as the cogs start whirring in our brains.

"Marxism?" I blurted out. Not sure where that came from.

"Got it in one," he smiles. "It's madness ... This attitude has become the norm in our country and you can thank the slow drip-drip of Marxism for it ... the long march through history ... Mark my words, I bet you that there will be no mention of the rally in the papers tomorrow."

That surprises me. "Really?" I say.

"Yes. Like I said, it goes against the narrative. If it had been a sea of union jacks and patriotic songs outside ... say ... Buckingham Palace after a royal event ... then the Daily Mail would have twenty pages dedicated to it. Because it's Tommy Robinson I guarantee ... there would not be a single mention ..."

We are flabbergasted.

"But ... all those people ... Trafalgar Square full up ... it's there before our eyes," says Derek.

"You'll see. Did you see many TV crews there, or reporters from the mainstream agencies, eh? No, I think not."

"There are going to be a lot of angry people tomorrow if this is so."

"Yes ... but better that for the establishment than actually allowing something new to disrupt the status quo."

"But they allow these pro-Palestinian demos and marches and they get mentioned in the papers."

"Yes ... true ...". Dave is pensive now. "But this is something new. A nation is rediscovering its ... identity. And those in

WHO AM I?

charge ... for whatever reason ... like it not one bit."

He gets up. He seems distracted. He says one more thing to us before leaving. "I'll be in touch. I'll email you in a day or two with my thoughts, once I've thought things through. I think it will all become clearer for you then."

19 We feel that we are coming to an end of our wanderings. We are quite exhausted with it all, it has been some roller coaster, with ups and downs and feelings of anticipation, excitement as well as dread. We don't have all the answers. Who could really have them in a situation that is ever-changing according to the whims of ... who knows? Do we really want to know? Not really. In business terms, *this is way above our pay grade!* Do we really care? Not sure. We ought to care, but we are unsure whether our caring about it will make any difference to something of this nature. This all becomes apparent one night when, just before bedtime, Derek asks me a direct question.

"Dawn?"

"Yes?"

"So ... do you have an answer to your question?"

"Which question?"

"You know ... the one you asked right at the beginning of all of this."

"Which is?" I am toying with him.

He holds my face between two outstretched palms and looks me straight in the eye.

"Who am I? ... that one!"

"Oh, "I reply, all innocently. "That one."

WHO AM I?

I pause as I compose my reply.

"Oh yes. I think I have the answer now, Derek. I am ... Dawn Courtney, happily married housewife and ... truth sleuth."

"Truth sleuth?"

"Yes ... I just made it up. Do you like it?"

"I think I do ... perhaps I should answer the same question, then."

"And your answer is?"

"I am ... Derek Courtney, the chap lucky enough to be married to the ... truth sleuth."

"And a truth sleuth too."

"I suppose ... I wonder where it's going to take us next, love?"

"Don't know ... let's sleep on it."

So we do.

WHO AM I?

INTERMISSION

Derek and Dawn are still on their journey of discovery and that is their story. Your story is a different one, but just as important. In our modern culture 'identity' has become a big issue but the feeling is that it is dictated to us rather than discovered by us. *Identity politics* is a real thing these days but, in the grand scheme of things, is it really important?

What is our identity anyway? Is there an ideal identity that we should aspire to, or is it best just to keep your head down and hope that the whole thing just goes away? And what about that group in Trafalgar Square? Are they rediscovering an 'identity' that has been lost and forgotten, even trampled on by those who wish to consign 'patriotism' to the past? Or is there still room for it? These are big questions, at a time when perhaps these questions are being revisited.

We are told that the best way of displaying your identity is by identifying with the vast array of victim groups out there, as long as they are 'approved' by the woke culture. We have already seen the full 'rainbow' of gender groups, well over a hundred of them. Then there are the groups identified by race, creed, religion, philosophy, politics etc. Groups are being added all of the time and the standard expectation is that we should be accepting of each group, even if they clash with other groups (as with the 'trans' women and the feminists) so that we can show our love and compassion for them. In reality all that happens is that what is emphasised is *the difference between the groups,* rather than what we have in common and this actually gives rise to distrust, division and hatred. One wonders if, perhaps, this is the actual objective of those who are promoting

WHO AM I?

this. A sober thought and one that we will now explore.

To understand the current state of affairs we need to go back in history, to the beginning of the last century …

PART TWO
A Matter of Identity
(by Podcast Steve)

20 Alice Bailey was an influential teacher in the early part of the 20th Century. She was hugely influential in the circles in which she moved, which unfortunately weren't nice places. This was because she was a theosophist, heavily into the occult and her writings were mainly of a "spiritual" nature and in fact, she claims that her key thoughts were dictated to her by a "Master of Wisdom", something distinctly unearthly. Her abiding aim was to see a "unified" society governed by a "world religion". She was one of the main forerunners of what we now call the New Age movement.

In 1948 she unleashed a ten-point plan, designed to wrench society away from its Christian roots. These points were so "far out" as to be unthinkable at the time - but reading them now is to see a description of where our world is in the UK and the West. It is also a huge indictment of modern society.

Point #1: Take God and prayer out of the education system.

Point #2: Reduce parental authority over the children.

Point #3: Destroy the traditional Judeo-Christian family structure.

Point #4: Make abortion legal and make it easy.

Point #5: Make divorce easy and legal, free people from the concept of marriage for life.

Point #6: Make homosexuality an alternative lifestyle.

Point #7: Debase art, make it run mad.

Point #8: Use media to promote and change mindset.

WHO AM I?

Point #9: Create an interfaith movement.

Point #10: Get governments to make all these [points] law and get the church to endorse these changes.

Alice Bailey said *"The Church must change its doctrine and accommodate the people by accepting these things and put them into its structures and systems."*

This is all happening as we speak. Her ten points were horribly accurate and prophetic. We now see a fulfillment of Alice Bailey's seventy-year-old plan for the breakdown of Christian society.

And no one has really noticed, because people don't care, they are too busy "living their lives" to stop and think about how they are living their lives, and what rules are there for living. We blindly trust society to draw us along ... and we usually call this "progress".

So how did this happen?

21 We begin our story with a failed global economic theory. This is the fruit of the mind of the German, Karl Marx, in the mid-19th Century. His basic teaching, *Marxism*, was a critique of Western capitalism, seeing it as a struggle between the ruling classes, who own the means of production and the working classes, who own nothing but their own bodies and who, for a standard wage, do the labour that enables the rich to get richer. In Marx's view, this system was unstable and would result in the working classes, as a result of a growth in self-realisation, rising up against their oppressors and creating a classless *communist* society, where everyone is 'equal'. They would do this through revolution, rather than evolution, so it was a philosophy of direct action and violent outcomes.

WHO AM I?

So, did theory ever become fact? Certainly not in his lifetime, though his theories were starting to stir things up in Germany and Russia by the time of his death in 1883. His greatest legacy though, is a bad one, with tens of millions of people dying as a result of various implementations of his theories, beginning with the Russian Revolution of 1917.

The First World War was a great disappointment for Communists and Marxists, as they fully expected the working classes to break the shackles of nationalism and refuse to fight for their country. They had grossly miscalculated, not anticipating the hold of patriotism for one's country above all and the 'rightness of their cause' as dictated by their Christian upbringing. For the Marxist theoreticians, the working classes had let themselves down and betrayed their class, the only success being the Bolsheviks in Russia, who followed the script, but consequently consigned their country to decades of totalitarian tyranny.

After the war, a group of these Marxist theoreticians in Germany began a re-evaluation of their philosophy, in the light of its failure to galvanise the working classes in Western Europe, who weren't revolting enough for their liking! *The Institute of Social Research* was founded, in Frankfurt Germany, in 1923. It was more commonly known as the *Frankfurt School.*

It is at this point that interpretive history forks into two, with two entirely different stories regarding the aims of this institution. There's the traditional, safe, view ... and there's the *other one.*

The safe view is supplied by the (supposedly) independent editors at Wikipedia. Here's how they introduce it:

"The Frankfurt School is a school of thought in sociology and critical philosophy. It is associated with the Institute for Social Research founded

101

WHO AM I?

at Goethe University Frankfurt in 1923. Formed during the Weimar Republic during the European interwar period, the first generation of the Frankfurt School was composed of intellectuals, academics, and political dissidents dissatisfied with the contemporary socio-economic systems of the 1930s: namely, capitalism, fascism, and communism. The Frankfurt theorists proposed that existing social theory was unable to explain the turbulent political factionalism and reactionary politics, such as Nazism, of 20th-century liberal capitalist societies. Also critical of Marxism–Leninism as a philosophically inflexible system of social organization, the School's critical-theory research sought alternative paths to social development. What unites the disparate members of the School is a shared commitment to the project of human emancipation, theoretically pursued by an attempted synthesis of the Marxist tradition, psychoanalysis, and empirical sociological research."

This conjures up an image of a cosy inwardly-looking academic think-tank, funded as a vanity project by a politically-minded left-leaning philanthropist.

The 'other' view is loaded with dynamite because it places the Frankfurt School at the heart of a massive, covert conspiracy, churning out not just theory, but a plan – a long march – for the implementation of its objectives, however long this may take, a plan that is *finding fulfilment every day in our modern world and seems to be the vehicle for implementing Alice Bailey's nefarious plan.*

So, one could either place the Frankfurt School at the heart of a conspiracy to bring down Western Civilisation as we know it, or one could insist that the real conspiracy is to *believe* that the Frankfurt School is at the heart of a conspiracy to bring down Western Civilisation as we know it. So it is either a real thing or just a fantasy believed by a bunch of cranks!

Well, then, call me a crank as I believe that that is where the

WHO AM I?

evidence leads. The main reason why many cannot bring themselves to agree with this view is that it reads like a plot of a Dan Brown or Frederick Forsyth novel. I have to admit that the conclusions derived from the clear evidence seem to be *downright unbelievable*. But that doesn't make it untrue.

22 So, here are the facts in summary form, which will then be unpacked. The eggheads at the Frankfurt School, by bringing in techniques from other disciplines, such as the psychoanalytical theories of Sigmund Freud, *re-invented Marxism*, taking it from the realms of economics (the battle of the classes) and into the very fabric of Western society, where the oppressors are not so much the ruling classes but rather the very institutions of Western culture. With the rise of Nazi Germany, they relocated to New York, based at Columbia University and there was born the new discipline of *Cultural Marxism*.

And there it is, *Cultural Marxism*. Proof of the divergence of views on this is demonstrated if you look at its entry in Wikipedia – there isn't one! Even 'fairies' have a Wikipedia entry and everyone knows they don't exist! Instead, you are redirected to a page labelled *Cultural Marxism Conspiracy Theory.* So, Wikipedia editors have *nailed their colours to their mast –* labelling everyone who delves into this issue as conspiracy theorists - and, by doing so, have ironically exhibited a key trait of practitioners of Cultural Marxism, *censorship without discussion.* More of this later as we go deeper into our subject.

Continuing our overview, how on earth were these academics going to be able to introduce their views into society? Being centred at a pliable university campus, their initial strategy was through academia. To pull in the intellectuals they formulated *Critical Theory*, a simple system disguised as a complex one to

WHO AM I?

hide its true intentions. *Critical Theory?* Where have we heard this term before? University social science departments are infected with it these days. It has now become mainstream, as a testament to the success of the infiltration of Cultural Marxism, something that 'supposedly' doesn't exist!

Even its Wikipedia page admits that the article *may be too technical for most readers to understand.* In a nutshell it states that ideology is the principal obstacle to human liberation. In other words, it is saying that our Judeo-Christian heritage and foundations are stopping us from being free! This all sounds very 'hippyish' and it may come as no surprise that the alternative culture of the 1960s was birthed by the minds of the Frankfurt School. I did warn you that we are going to venture into some very strange places.

Our story begins in 1930 when the school started formulating its controversial strategies under the leadership of its new director, Max Horkheimer. Under this new leadership, the Frankfurt School was to move away from academic concerns to a wider remit, *critical social research,* which involved an integration of the social sciences, a significant development. Key academics brought in to follow this path were Erich Fromm, the psychoanalyst, Theodor Adorno, the sociologist and Herbert Marcuse, the academic philosopher. Things were now going to get a little tasty. Fromm worked with Horkheimer on finding connections between the theories of Marx and Sigmund Freud. The area of attack here was social change and, in particular, the *role of the family in society.* These men were arrogantly going to interfere with a system that has worked perfectly well for thousands of years. To further this, Adorno later became involved too, working towards a goal of the reinterpretation of the family unit. At all times, ideas were filtered through Marxist principles, using 'dialectical

WHO AM I?

mediation', whatever that may be.

In 1935, when being a Communist was not exactly the best career choice for thriving in Nazi Germany, the School was moved to Columbia University in New York. Two years later Horkheimer published the manifesto of the School, *Traditional and Critical Theory*. In 1941 Horkheimer moved to Los Angeles, close to the film industry, later followed by Marcuse and Adorno. Five years later he returned to Germany, leaving the other two behind to continue their work in the USA.

For laymen such as you and me, the best way to try and understand their approach and their motivations, one needs to get some sort of handle on 'Critical Theory', the driving force behind all of their ideas. The simplest way of looking at it is that it is a system where *everything is there to be criticised and deconstructed*. It doesn't offer solutions to fill in the gap of what they may have destroyed, it is simply a wrecking ball bludgeoning its way through the certainties of Western Civilisation. One basic principle was to *reject the notion of objectivity in knowledge*. This is highly significant and lays down the roots of the relativism that is one of the key drivers in the Western world today, and, in fact, the whole of *postmodernism* – the predominant driver of Western society - flows from this one statement. It answers the question, *what is truth?* with the answer ... *whatever you want it to be*. They qualify this by suggesting that historical and social factors need to be taken into account, including a consideration of the situation itself and who is the one perceiving it. It leads to the situation of politicians and philosophers telling us what to believe. No room here for absolute truth. Although there's a lot deeper one can go in what is, by its nature a dense philosophical system, it is sufficient for our understanding to consider the millions of words written on this just as commentary, and to hold on to the

WHO AM I?

single defining statement – *to reject the notion of objectivity in knowledge – a rejection of absolute truth*. Everything else flows from this ... and it started to flow in the 1950s.

23 Theodor Adorno kicked off the 1950s with a book, *the Authoritarian Personality*, a hugely influential book in the subsequent years. The book was a wolf in sheep's clothing. Ostensibly written to help quash the re-emergence of *Fascism*, it downplayed the Marxism that inspired it, to make it palatable for those who believed in democracy. It introduced the *F-Scale* (F standing for pre-Fascist personality), as a way of determining authoritarian propensities, on the premise that Fascism is the worst kind of authoritarianism and it can be detected early in a child's development, with sexual repression a factor! The Frankfurt School's dabbling with Freud can be seen here and Adorno reveals his true intentions by declaring that Fascism can result from religion and conventional middle-class values concerning family, sex and society. According to the book, budding fascists can be those who believe in obedience and respect for authority, or have negative views on homosexuality, or who have a high view of personal honour.

What is happening here? You can understand the fear people had that Fascism may rise again and who better to teach the American social scientists than a German academic? Remembering the goal of the Frankfurt School concerning the family and Western civilisation, we now have the germ of an idea that those who are brought up to have a high view of both ... *possibly have fascist tendencies!* This idea is going to come back and haunt as all, as this story progresses.

Moving on to Herbert Marcuse, he agreed with Adorno that Fascism can be traced back to psychological and sexual

WHO AM I?

repression but then he switched things round. He stated that the good guys, the *anti-fascists,* would be the opposite, people defined by psychological and sexual liberation! He introduced this all in his first influential book, *Eros and Civilisation,* published in 1955. Here he made proposals that were eventually to ignite an explosion in the following decade. He suggested that the prevailing technological, capitalist society traps people by limiting their sexual libido, turning sex into a commodity and using religion and morality to suppress these natural instincts, through its promotion of monogamy and aversion to sexual perversion.

Let it all hang out, proclaimed Marcuse. *Suppressed sexuality is for fascists!* It should be no surprise, when the permissive sixties took on these ideas and an aged German philosopher became a sex guru for a generation, even coining the slogan. *Make love not war.*

So, what have we learned so far? That, *allegedly,* the propensity for Fascism is limited to those from a traditional Christian family background and that only rampant sexuality can thwart these impulses. Isn't it amazing how a German accent and a book full of indecipherable concepts can convince the gullible that right is wrong and wrong is right. Remember, the chief objective of Critical Theory was the denial of absolute truth. Adorno and Marcuse are playing around dangerously with the truth and the amazing thing is that not only were otherwise sensible people listening to them, but that these skewed ideas would gain traction in the subsequent years.

By the end of the 1950s, the subtle influence of Cultural Marxism was beginning to bite. This was reflected in the shifting emphasis in the films produced by Hollywood, away from those reinforcing the Judeo-Christian bedrock of stable

WHO AM I?

family relationships and wholesome living and towards the situation we find ourselves in today, where even family films depict casual sex, adultery, criminality and a dubious moral base. The 'envelope' is continually being pushed, with barriers of good taste and cultural taboos being broken continuously, *as if this is a good thing and an end in its own right*. They call this 'progress' and we are going to see this term pop up again and again and used by those who feel they are part of a positive move of progression. They call themselves 'progressives' and one wonders *what actually they are progressing towards,* though it is clear what they are leaving behind. Where will this end? It is very troubling and we really need to fear for our children and grandchildren as to what kind of 'culture' they are going to inherit from us.

24 There is much rose-tinted nostalgia regarding the 1960s, even among those who were not even born yet. If there was one man who did more to create the framework for the major shifts during that decade then it was not John Lennon or Elvis Presley or Timothy Leary or Martin Luther King or John Kennedy or Bob Dylan, but it was our sixty-something German Marxist academic, *Herbert Marcuse himself.*

Critical Theory, the driving force of Cultural Marxism, is all about tearing down institutions that form the bedrock of our culture, with a particular strategy of re-defining the family. It is purely destructive and is very much tied in with the Marxist ideology of control of the collective and the squashing of the individual. It is *'1984* personified', interesting as George Orwell was a socialist writing at a time when the Frankfurt School was beginning to make its sinister inroads. It is also interesting that the 1960s birthed the *counter-culture* and we can now begin to grasp that this was not initiated by a bunch of idealistic hippies,

WHO AM I?

but there were other forces at play here.

Herbert Marcuse, sex guru. Through the message of his increasingly read *Eros and Civilisation*, he was subtly declaring the hidden message, *prove you ain't a potential fascist, get laid!* Remember, his philosophy, shared with his co-patriot Theodor Adorno, identified Fascism with sexual morality, family values and a Christian lifestyle. How better can you cleanse yourself from any unsociable right-wing tendencies than to indulge your fleshly appetites! This was aided by the advent of the birth control pill at the beginning of the decade, so significant that it was referred to as just 'the Pill', the chemical gateway to guilt-free sex. And, in the case of the odd 'accident', convenient abortions were made legally available as the result of the Abortion Act in the UK in 1967. Interestingly, convenience abortions were made legal as early as 1919 in Soviet Russia.

Marcuse's influence on the 1960s was profound. For him, the traditions of the family and of a Christian lifestyle were repressive and worth overthrowing, as was any adherence to objective truth. Everything is up to the individual, breaking free of shackles, a philosophy worryingly but significantly similar to the Satanist creed of Aleister Crowley, *do what you wilt shall be the whole of the law.* The Children of the 1960s were free to romp around and indulge themselves, but still benefited from the affluence provided for them by their hard-working parents, who had largely triumphed over the post-war austerity measures by providing their children with a safe, secure upbringing. And what was the payback? Rather than rebels without a cause, they were *rebels with big cars.*

But Marcuse had a lot more in his locker. He'd only just got started! In 1964 he wrote *One Dimensional Man*, described by Douglas Kellner as *one of the most subversive books of the 20th*

WHO AM I?

Century. It was the book that really put Marcuse on the map. Traditional Marxists and capitalists hated it, but the growing band of young political activists loved it. In the book he attacked the American capitalist society for reducing human beings to consumers at the mercy of advertisers, with their freedom curtailed by the ever-manipulated need to carry on consuming. They are reduced, in his view, to being 'one dimensional' in their thoughts and attitudes. I see nothing fundamentally wrong in this assessment of the wrongs of consumerism, as it's really not the best way of ordering our lives. It's Marcuse's solution that sets him apart from most of his contemporaries.

He offered a new way of looking at the world in his subsequent writings. He was very much for direct action, political propaganda, any means to wake up the people and mobilise them against the forces of capitalism. A later book, *An Essay on Liberation,* was an outline for liberation, for action, for revolution. It was a handbook taken up by a new species of protester that was birthed out of an existing species. Welcome to the *New Left.*

The 'Old Left' were the original political left wing in the West, such as The Labour Party in the UK. They were typified mainly by the blue-collar workers, the working class, who just wanted a fair wage and food on the table. Out of this movement came the Welfare State in the UK after the Second World War. In general terms their politics didn't travel further than a mutual concern for working people wherever they may be. This is the Labour party of Keir Hardie, Harold Wilson and Denis Healey and others. Safe, comfortable and traditionally British. This was the party my father voted for, people he – an ordinary working man (taxi driver) – felt were a safe pair of hands to look after his interests. In the USA they were the Democrats, typified by Franklin D Roosevelt and Harry Truman, with a sprinkling of

WHO AM I ?

Communists beavering away intent on disruption, particularly through the Unions.

25 The *New Left* were the angry young upstarts, not so interested in economics, but much more interested in the culture of the day. This was reminiscent of the changes in Marxism itself, with Marx and the old guard concentrating on economic theory, but with the new guard at the Frankfurt school re-envisioning it in cultural terms. The New Left had less to say about social class and more to say about the issues of the day such as feminism, racism, civil rights, drugs, the environment and the peace movement. In fact, *perhaps they had too much to say?*

Leaders of this political offshoot in the USA included men such as Jerry Rubin and Albert Hoffman, who represented the 'hippie' fringe. Hoffman was quoted thus:

"Once one has experienced LSD, existential revolution, fought the intellectual game-playing of the individual in society, of one's identity, one realizes that action is the only reality; not only reality but morality as well. It exists in the head. I am the Revolution".

Of course, not all 'revolutionaries' were drug-fuelled, spiritually confused, student dropouts. Those who were into revolution looked overseas and made idols out of Marxist tyrants, whose crimes hadn't quite caught up with them yet, men such as Che Guevara, Fidel Castro and Ho Chi Minh. Certainly, the image of Che the revolutionary was probably the defining image of the times, adorning many a student bedroom or t-shirt, the fierce 'freedom fighter' who was, in actuality, a ruthless mass-murderer who ponged a bit (he rarely washed).

The New Left was a 'broad church', a clearing house for young discontents with fire in their bellies, whether they were left-liberal, socialist, or anarchist, whether they were drawn into

WHO AM I?

one of the many offshoot subcultures, such as gay rights or the pacifists at *The Campaign for Nuclear Disarmament* (CND) in the UK (Jeremy Corbyn was active in this as a schoolboy). They were united simply through the new freedom they felt they had been given to protest against the 'Old ways'. In the UK the New Left was pioneered by such men as Stuart Hall (who introduced 'cultural studies' into British colleges), Edward Thompson (one of the prime movers of CND in the 1950s) and Raymond Williams (a Marxist philosopher).

And, at the centre of this all, quietly pulling the strings, either indirectly through his books, or directly through direct action, was Herbert Marcuse, *the acknowledged father of the New Left*. He had an aggressive distaste for the capitalist American society that had provided him with a comfortable living. The key year was 1968, when theory became action, when the whole world was rocked, the year of the student protests (just a few months after their 'summer of love', how fickle the youth are!)

These were the young turks of the New Left snarling at the western world. In May 1968, France was virtually brought to a standstill, with general strikes and occupations of factories and universities. Some politicians actually feared a civil war or revolution and this was said to be a cultural turning point in the country's history. The waves of protests had swept through West Berlin, Rome, London, Paris and many cities in the USA, as well as other places. What exactly were these people, mainly students, protesting about? It was a general old moan and one old leftie (Chris Harman), looking back to that year declared *"suddenly it seemed that the coming together of many different acts of revolt could overturn an exploitative and oppressive society in its totality.*

Exploitative? Oppression? We can sense the presence of a certain old German philosopher here, can't we? During the 1960s and

WHO AM I?

1970s Herbert Marcuse cheerfully welcomed invitations to speak at many of the centres of protest, the universities. During one particular French student occupation some leaders put on a seminar entitled *'journee marcusienne'*. In Rome placards declared, "Marx, Mao, Marcuse". But there was an even more sinister development here. He was happy to accept invitations to speak ... but insisted that invitations should *not* be offered to others, those he particularly disagreed with. He said that they can't be allowed to persist in their misguided and evil ways, giving birth to a slogan that is relevant today, *no free speech for fascists*. Out of this idea comes one of the central themes of the political correctness that increasingly plagues us today. Let us investigate ...

Here's how Marcuse thought this through. He began well by admitting that classical virtues such as tolerance and free speech are desirable. But, he says, our society is divided between the oppressors, who have the power and the 'disenfranchised' who have little. So there should be little tolerance extended to the oppressors, but rather it should only be extended to 'groups that are being discriminated against'. In his own words he was advocating *"the systematic withdrawal of tolerance towards regressive and repressive opinions"*. And who are the purveyors of these opinions? According to Marcuse they were the groups and movements promoting chauvinism, aggressive policies, discrimination on the grounds of race and religion or which oppose the extension of public services, such as social services and medical care. In his view this just about included anyone who didn't share his particular Marxist view of society. This also included restrictions on certain teachings in universities and intolerance of any movements from the 'right-wing', which led to the already-mentioned chant, *no free speech for fascists*.

WHO AM I?

26 This is where it gets very sinister, because *who provides the definition of 'a fascist'?* We are reminded of Theodor Adorno's definition, in *the Authoritarian Personality*, endorsed by Marcuse, that *Fascism can result from religion and conventional middle-class values on family, sex and society.* Something has been turned on its head here. Marcuse and his ilk are implying that free speech and tolerance are only to be extended to those who *don't fit their particular definition of Fascism* – basically anyone who is not from a traditional, middle-class Christian background!

What Marcuse is advocating is to give licence to those (loosely) of the New Left to use any tactic they can think of to oppress and repress their opposition, basically those of a Conservative, Judeo-Christian inclination, now renamed 'fascists'. And this could involve direct action, as anything is justified for the self-proclaimed 'social warriors on the side of peace and liberation'.

So, we now have the 'set up', the first seeds of the madness that pervades our Western cultural life. We will next look at the journey between then and now.

27 There is an aspect of our Western culture that has been creeping relentlessly into the 'big picture'. It has been the butt of many jokes in past years and considered a harmless oddity, *but not any more.* It now rules the roost and it has very sinister intentions. It went by the name of *political correctness* but is now better known as *woke ideology.*

It didn't just pop out of nowhere, as a whim of an over-zealous civil servant. It is the outcome of a 'long march' through recent history and is nothing less than a strategy to undermine and destroy the bedrocks of Western civilisation, the Judeo-Christian framework, with particular emphasis on the traditional family unit. It is the legacy of Marcuse, Adorno and

WHO AM I?

others from the Frankfurt School and it has carried the toxic 'spirit of the 60s' through to the modern day, modifying itself as it does so. It is very much in the spirit of Cultural Marxism, as it takes its core beliefs and assumptions from the Critical Theory insistence on the rejection of the notion of objectivity in knowledge, *a rejection of absolute truth.*

But this beast has a bite that is fatal. Consider Tim Farron, the political leader of the Liberal Democrats in the UK who was driven out of his job through assumptions about his views on the LGBTIQ+ agenda, or Walt Tutka, a substitute teacher in the USA who was fired for handing a Bible to a student. Political correctness acquired this bite by worming its agenda into government legislation, and if you are wondering how this can happen then we are going to need a history lesson. How did the counter-culture of the 60s become such a driving force in the culture of today?

The central thrust of Cultural Marxism is the promotion of a 'victim culture', of building a narrative whereby all of the world's ills are the fault of the prevailing culture, specifically white men working from within a Christian context. Critical Theory began to roll out a series of 'causes', centring on those deemed to be 'victims', such as black people, women, homosexuals, native Americans etc. There seems to be a worthiness in this until one realises that these causes were just part of the context of Cultural Marxism. Anyone who dared criticise this process is condemned variously as homophobic, misogynists, Islamophobic, racist, sexist and so on. Most of all – in the legacy of Marcuse – they are labelled as 'fascists'. You may remember the anarchist 'Rick', played by Rick Mayall in the 1990s sitcom *The Young Ones*. When stuck for words, this character - a comedy parody of a young 'new leftie' - would scream 'fascist' at whoever was annoying him. This was an

WHO AM I?

ironically accurate depiction of the New Left's reflex response to any criticism of its activities.

So, let's reword the gist of that last paragraph, to consolidate its impact. Whereas traditional Marxism set up the ruling class, the capitalists, as the aggressors and the working class as the victims, Cultural Marxism takes the same pattern but tweaks it. In place of the ruling class, we have the traditional Western 'Christian' society as aggressor and any number of 'marginalised' groups as 'victim'. One key idea here is that the aggressor is never allowed any leeway, any shred of compassion, or any way of redeeming itself. It must be destroyed. Surely, we see here the primacy of the ideology rather than a real concern for the 'victims' who are being 'defended'? This may seem a cynical attitude for me to take, but imagine if I am right on this, how cynical it is to perpetuate an ideology that creates conflict for their own ends?!

Now here is something important. We may now have some sort of handle on Cultural Marxism, but what about *Cultural Marxists,* who are they? It is important that we don't judge those caught up in this mindset, the 'victims', as Cultural Marxists, as they are simply actors in the drama. Who, actually, *are pulling the strings?* Who, actually, are the Cultural Marxists, those who *are* setting the agenda and promoting it? A difficult one, as we may never actually find out, though there is probably many a university professor or social commentator, who may fit this bill to a certain extent. We may never find the answer to this question.

So, for Cultural Marxists, a Christian *can never be a victim,* even in the case of the persecuted Church in Muslim countries (is there such word as Christianophobia?). *Israel and the Jews* sadly are not allowed any 'victim' status under this New Left thinking

116

WHO AM I?

(witness the inability of Jeremy Corbyn to acknowledge, let alone deal with, anti-Semitism in the UK Labour Party in 2018 and the current issues that the Labour still has over Israel). Similarly, a *white heterosexual male* can also never be a victim. Has anyone heard of men's rights or male emancipation in an age when a feminine spirit seems to be holding ever-increasing sway? Another key idea, equally important, is that the 'victim' is chosen by the Cultural Marxists themselves and held in some sort of hierarchy (with 'multiculturalism' or 'ethnic minorities' at the top at present). The 'victims' don't get a say in this, unless they themselves are Cultural Marxists, which is unlikely. It is 'Big Brother' gone ... mad, mad, mad!

A telling quote of where we are now supposedly comes from the well-known French philosopher, Voltaire:

"To learn who rules over you, simply find out who you are not allowed to criticize."

It is a brave man (or woman) who dares to test this one out in the current climate.

28 There was a quirky star-studded film from gentler times. It was called *It's a mad, mad, mad, mad world* and was basically a treasure hunt spanning California, with lots of car chases and jolly japes. Yet its title may have been prophetic as the world today is truly mad - and not in a jolly sense. The warning signs may have been the Brexit/Trump 'double whammy' a few years back, but the liberal and leftist establishment has fought back, with interest, and the average citizen in the West whose mind has not been jellified by overdoses of reality TV, immersive digital entertainment and celebrity trivia must really wonder whether we have slipped into an alternate dimension.

Wasn't there a time where we had a spatial sense of the political

WHO AM I?

climate, when we knew what a far-left-winger was and when someone on the far-right was perhaps missing a few marbles. Both extremes were tolerated and kept within safe zones and far away from our comfortable lives ordered by middle-ground compromise politics. *There they are on the TV news, on their marches, with their abrasive banners and angry faces. Let them let off steam, it's of no relevance to me.*

How times have changed, as the mindset that governs these people has now wheedled itself into the mainstream and is very much affecting us all in different ways. We can blaspheme the Christian God to our heart's content, but we risk our livelihoods if we even hint at the n-word when referring to a black man. We live in a world where those on the far-left will defend militant Islam, despite the violent disdain offered back. Where the EU has an iron hand to punish 'human rights' crimes within its borders but ignores the most savage atrocities committed just beyond its borders. Where left-wingers would weep and wail over Palestine but ignore Syria, China, Sudan, Zimbabwe, Yemen, North Korea or the Congo. Where the far-left oppose far-right movements as long as they are run by white men, but actually often speak in favour of foreign far-right regimes, as long as they are anti-Western. Where leftist apologists point at the mass murder committed by right-wing dictators but conveniently ignore the far greater numbers killed at the hands of left-wing dictators, such as Stalin or Mao.

It used to be that the right-wing tended to support victims of Communism and dictatorships connected to Soviet Russia, whereas the left-wing supported the victims of Fascist regimes and right-wing dictatorships. For the far-left the goalposts have moved, *they would now treat as friend anyone who opposes Western democracy.* That is their over-riding narrative and it ensures that you wouldn't get them marching against the Islamic massacres

WHO AM I?

in Africa, or the murderous Syrian regime, but they would take to the London streets in their droves over the war in Gaza. You may remember at the time of the Gulf War that demonstrations were a-plenty against the actions of the Western coalition forces, but you would not see any on the streets in the years leading up to this, protesting against the evil genocidal regime of Saddam Hussein. Pic 'n' mix morality, indeed!

Yes, these are extreme views and this comes from the far-left agenda, rather than the more moderate liberals and it would be unfair to tar the latter with the murky brush of the former. The fact is that there are a myriad of viewpoints about a myriad of things and simple logic is not always followed, though deeply held prejudices tend to hold sway. This highlights the broad spectrum of views that span the political landscape from left to right, these days. *Politics has never been so complicated!*

It is interesting and significant that those people, nominally of the far-left, who embrace the 'Brave New World' ushered in by Cultural Marxism, proclaim themselves as *progressives*. They consider this homogenising of society and the stripping of individual freedoms as *progress*. Yet haven't we grown up with this concept, of society's forward trajectory, breaking down barriers and forging ahead, going by the name of 'progress'? We are fed the refrain, this is progress … *we've turned away from old superstitions / outdated rules of moral conduct / the restrictions of the patriarchal society.* It may be a forward trajectory for them, but for right-minded people (and not just Christians) it is simply a retreat from our true foundations.

29 There is an inconvenient, uncomfortable and unspoken truth here which makes sense to those of a forensic disposition. *There is really no difference between those of the far-left and the far-right, where it really matters.*

119

WHO AM I?

One may promote internationalism, over the nationalism of the other, *but they both boil down to the masses being controlled and abused by a murderous elite,* whether a Nazi Germany or a Communist world state.

It is a fact that, in terms of how these philosophies have been implemented, there is little difference between Fascism and Communism. They both worked together, usually against the liberal societies of the day, many times in the early to mid-20th Century, with a prime example being the (temporary) pact between Stalin and Hitler. The dark corridors of the human soul stretch out both to the left and to the right and, in the dark, both look pretty much the same. It has all become a blur and the world of politics has given birth to a whole swathe of political denominations. We can begin to appreciate the upheaval in the 2016 US elections, where the 'finish line' was contested by two candidates seemingly at home in the extreme expressions of their 'wing' of their party, leaving the average citizen having to choose the one who would do the least damage, rather than the one who would actually benefit the Nation. It was a no-win situation for the electorate and it seems that we have a repeat of the same scenario at the time of writing.

Perhaps the craziest (and saddest) spectacle has been the alliance between the left and the Islamists. The only thing they seem to have in common is their disdain or hatred for the Western culture (and, of course, the Jews) but this seems to outweigh the certainty that, if the Islamists ever succeed in building their caliphate in the UK, the first heads to roll (literally) would be the liberals, leftists, gays, feminists, atheists (and, of course, the Jews). Yet the left-wing can't bring itself to oppose them and would support them on campaigns and marches on whatever issue the Islamists choose. Hatred

WHO AM I?

outweighs everything, it seems, especially when it is dressed up in the language and actions of political correctness. Here is a real-life story to support this sad fact.

It was said to be the biggest child protection scandal in UK history. It was in Rotherham and, incredibly, it went on undetected for over twenty years and involved the systematic sexual abuse of over 1,400, mostly underage white girls, some as young as 12 years old. The group members, who have now been brought to justice, were of Pakistani Muslim origin and it is now being revealed that this may be the tip of a very sordid iceberg, with similar goings-on in other towns in the Midlands and the North of England. The tragedy of this is that it could have been nipped in the bud, but it wasn't, despite the police and the council being very aware of these activities very early on. At a House of Commons hearing into the case, three main reasons were given why this wasn't dealt with earlier:

1. Community relations – not wanting to be accused of racism, because of the fact that the perpetrators were predominantly Asian Muslims.

2. Prejudice and indifference to the victims, who were working-class girls (some in care homes), living on the margins of society.

3. Self-interest – the Labour council didn't want to lose votes from its largely ethnic electorate.

The overriding factor was *political correctness,* where the facade of 'multiculturalism' had to be maintained, despite the connection to Islamic culture that seemed to lay at the very heart of the case. Many of these South Asian young men were trapped in loveless arranged marriages and were taught that 'white girls' were fair game and were to be treated as subhuman. You will get a better flavour of the issues here from

WHO AM I?

a news item, regarding an outburst from Labour MP, Naz Shah, a close ally of Jeremy Corbyn. She spoke out against a fellow Labour MP, Sarah Champion, who had remarked that Britain *"had a problem with Pakistani men targeting vulnerable white girls"*. Despite new Pakistani grooming scandals being uncovered in Newcastle and other places, Shah had this to say about her fellow MP, that she used *"blanket racialised, loaded statements that stigmatised the Pakistani community"*. Corbyn, on his Facebook page, praised Shah and accused the newspaper that originally printed Champion's remarks of using *"Nazi-like terminology about a minority community"*.

Can you read between the lines here? Here we have the biggest child abuse scandal ever to happen in the UK and, rather than addressing the root causes of the scandal, the spokespeople of Cultural Marxism attempt to imply that 'victims' can't be perpetrators and anyone who believes otherwise is labelled with words like 'racist' and 'nazi'. Meanwhile there are 1,400 young girls with ruined lives and, no doubt, other groups of young men continuing the abuses elsewhere, secure in the (hopefully dwindling) protection of 'victim immunity'.

30 Where else does political correctness scratch and tear at the fabric of sensible living? Well, certainly at many of those closeted laboratories of skewed thinking, the Universities. The University of California is such a place. Students have to be very careful what they say, for fear of offending the 'thought police' (rather than the minorities who are supposedly offended but, in reality, mostly couldn't give a fig!). Here are some no-nos:

"There is only one race, the human race". This is supposedly offensive to 'people of colour' as it 'denies their ethnic experience and history'.

WHO AM I?

"America is the land of opportunity" implies that 'people of colour' are lazy, incompetent and need to work harder?!

Welcome to the world of *micro-aggression*. These are casual remarks that you and I may make out of innocence, but which could be taken by others as an offence. These are the triggers that feed the political correctness culture and, despite the claim of ushering in a society suffused with brotherly love, actually create far more division and strife, by perpetuating a culture of perceived victimhood.

With its accent on 'victims', Cultural Marxism has even convinced some in the University system that they themselves fall into this category, such is the power of this insidious philosophy. A former law student at a major university is suing it for loss of earnings because she wasn't allowed to sit her exams in a private room due to chronic anxiety and, as a result graduated a year later than expected. She is suing for the wages she would have earned in that past year! Other cases abound, including a student who so objected to receiving any kind of criticism that she felt that if she attained any grade lower than a First, it would be the fault of others. The *National Union of Students* (NUS) has even tried to ban cheering and clapping because it could cause anxiety to the more sensitive students. Where on earth has the bulldog spirit gone that made this nation great? Where is the 'stiff upper lip'? Have people basically changed that much in a couple of generations? Probably not, but there seems to be little resistance to the life being sucked out of our current generation through the destructive influence of mind-numbing media, trivia being pumped into our brains ... and the subtle machinations and restrictions to our personal freedoms through political correctness (and its cousin, *health and safety*). Not for nothing, it seems, is the current generation becoming increasingly

WHO AM I?

dubbed "the snowflake generation".

So, you now see the mess we in the West are in. Perhaps you are puzzled how this craziness could have crept up on us. Wasn't Communism defeated in the 1980s with the collapse of the Soviet Empire? Hasn't Russia opened up more to the forces of democracy and capitalism? The actual story is very different to what you may have been fed in the media and through academia. This may sound like the mutterings of a conspiracy buff but before you judge me, I need to ask a very important question:

What if academia and the media and even Hollywood have fed us *their* version of the truth, rather than the *actual truth?* What I am not saying is that we have to question everything but, in order to test the hypothesis that there may have been some 'spin' to news and events, we have to follow the evidence. If there had been a proven left-wing bias in academia, media and Hollywood since the war, then we must find at least some of the evidence we need.

Academia may prove the death of us all! It was the academics who devised and promoted the subversive objectives of Cultural Marxism, it has been the academics (aka. theologians) who serve to obscure the simple faith in Jesus, and it is apparently the Islamic scholars who justify and encourage the nihilistic death-squads through their interpretations of their sacred texts. In 1972 Dr Myron L. Fox ran a series of lectures entitled *Mathematical Game Theory as applied to Physical Education* to university graduates, who were then asked to rate his performance in a questionnaire. He was marked highly, 80% of them rated him as well organised and said he stimulated their thinking. They lived to regret this as the whole thing was a hoax, Fox was an actor who just read out rearranged sentences

WHO AM I ?

from a *Scientific American* article! The talk was full of contradictory statements and double talk but this was all overlooked and their integrity was sacrificed at the altar of the illusion of intellectual authority.

The reason why this is relevant is that our modern politically correct culture is being fed by babbling academics, mainly from American university arts and social studies departments and particularly those who specialise in the latest cultural 'theory', whether it addresses race, agenda, identity or religion. Many have been sucked into the 'Professor's new clothes' and are far too sophisticated to realise that their beloved academic is wandering around butt naked! But this was no joke, because, incredibly, some of this 'theory' eventually became 'practice'. The focus was on elevating victims of past injustices into a position of such dominance that any criticism of this would be met with hostility and alienation. From a (worthy) starting point of addressing victimisation of women, gays and blacks, 'theory' elevated each into a category of its own, that couldn't be criticised or challenged by using universally held criteria of argument or debate. Each became a narrative of its own, protected by the relativism of the age (what may be right for you may not necessarily be so for me) and to this list was added new categories, such as suicide bombing, Hindu wife burning, female circumcision or ... the rights of gays to promote their ideologies through the talents of Christian bakers. Those on the outside are not allowed to make judgements as the Cultural Marxist narrative is free to decide what was right or wrong and no-one else had the right to comment.

31 If you do happen to clash with this 'narrative' then expect to be smeared by accusations of being a racist, a nazi, a fascist, a homophobe, Islamophobe,

WHO AM I?

even an antisemite (if it suits the 'narrative'). You will get special attention if you are perceived as a member of the 'imperialistic' class i.e. a white, middle-class male Christian. You will note that there are no 'isms' or 'phobias' to protect anyone who is white, middle-class, male or a Christian! You are an enemy by definition of Cultural Marxism, unless you join the band of 'useful idiots', a term coined by Lenin, referring to those he and his fellow Communists were able to cynically manipulate to further their own ends.

I was compelled to observe the anti-Trump London rally, when the US President visited in July 2018. It is interesting how a single cause can bring together people from such a diverse selection of humanity, but it is frightening to observe that what united many of them was pure hatred and that their expression of this hatred were chants and slogans of the most offensive, personal and degrading nature. This was not unity in diversity over a just cause, it was a spiteful expression of ignorance. This latter observation was reinforced when a small group of pro-Trump supporters confronted them and attempted to engage with them, only to be met with a stream of invective, mindless chants ... and silence. When push came to shove, most demonstrators hadn't a clue about the issues behind the rally, they came for the entertainment alone ... and many even brought their kids along. This is what Cultural Marxism has done to our population, it is beginning to strip out any semblance of independent thought.

This is the driving force of our politically correct culture ... and it is certainly no joke any more! So how does all of this affect us now, in 21st Century Britain? It's incredible that the fruits of Critical Theory now surround us. Hatred and suspicion have triumphed over love and collaboration. The current Labour Party has provided a channel of prejudice, masquerading as

WHO AM I?

tolerance, our future sacrificed on the altar of the very real wrongs of the past. Yet their arch-enemy, the Tories, are in the thrall of the same Cultural Marxism. There is no forgiveness, history has frozen with no possibility of a clean slate. Instead, there is just recrimination and restrictions. There is no real hope for our society if Cultural Marxism is allowed to continue unchecked.

128

PART THREE

Which Kingdom?

(by Podcast Dave)

32 Dear Derek & Dawn,

Thanks so much for being such willing companions on my recent adventure. I am still reeling over the implications of what we saw and heard in Trafalgar Square. As expected, the print media on Sunday was largely silent apart from a short piece in *The Times* mocking the fact that Tommy Robinson has been arrested over a film he showed at the event, breaking an injunction over its viewing. The folk attending the rally were described thus, "the crowd flew St George's Cross flags, drank beer and sported teal Reform UK rosettes." Perhaps we were at a different rally?

I am not one for propagating 'conspiracy theories' but when one is an eyewitness to an event that is either airbrushed away or is presented to the public in a way that shatters any pretence of fair reporting, then my antenna starts to tingle. What we experienced was a glimpse of a Britain that many wish to consign to the past and I ask the question, why should they do so? It is a Britain that is not defined by 'victim groups' in its midst, that need to be celebrated and apologised to. The Russell Square counter-rally was more a protest on behalf of victim groups (Palestinians, refugees, LGBT+) and who felt that chanting 'Nazi scum' in the direction of Trafalgar Square was a satisfying contribution to cultural discourse. What we saw was an expression of hatred towards those they oppose vastly outweighing any real compassion they may have to those groups they claim to represent. For example, real love towards the Gazans would be to demand that Hamas release the hostages rather than creating targets out of their own citizens.

WHO AM I?

Instead, they feel justified in expressing their hatred of Israel and wish genocide upon the Jewish people. This is very skewed thinking.

At Trafalgar Square we saw a Britain that has, in reality, moved from its 'colonial' past, despite what these 'others' tell you. Yes, it is not a Britain that celebrates Middle East terrorist groups, militant faiths that wish to impose their values on us, or those who are gender confused but, instead, it is a Britain that tolerates those who are different and invites them to unite with us. There were many black people at the rally. I'm sure there were gay people there and Muslims, as well as those of other faiths and inclinations. But these were people who, primarily, would say that they are proud to be British, *first of all*. There are more of these people than could be imagined and a solution to the cultural tensions that exists is for these people to come to the fore and say, *"brother and sister, let's work together and build a better society"* rather than follow the party line that so many have been lured into that says, *"brother and sister, let's show how proudly different we are and punish any who will not celebrate us."* This is victim politics and it is tearing our country apart.

What we see is a country unsure any more of its identity. Pride should be in our nation, not in our sexuality or muscular faith. We are troubled by what we see as Islamic incursions in our daily life, whether it is the disruption and noise of a pro-Palestinian demonstration, the rise of naked antisemitism, focussed on the goings-on in Gaza, the child grooming scandals, the illegal migrant crisis or the meddling in our political system with an overt strategy to get Muslims to vote for other Muslims, or at least for those who are deemed supporters of Palestinian issues. This all smacks of a subversive force within our nation seeking to destabilise it. There undoubtedly is one and, although it uses militant Islam as its ammunition, those

WHO AM I?

wielding the guns are most definitely from the far left, as we saw in Russell Square. Unfortunately, we are not served by a media or a government that acts on this this but would rather follow this destabilising narrative that would cause many to tell me to *get a life*, go with the flow and stop being a peddler of conspiracies.

The really sad thing about this is that the majority of Muslims have bought into the idea of British nationhood. They understand the values of raising their families, working hard to better themselves, support local football teams, join community groups (and not just Muslim ones), turn out for Royal occasions, vote according to conviction, and just want to be a part of a truly multicultural landscape. Here they are joined by Hindus, Sikhs, Jews, Buddhists and others of faith or no faith, as well as those of 'different' sexualities. Their primary identity is thus defined. This is surely the dream of an authentic multicultural Britain, but it seems that those who proclaim it the most are the same people who are subverting it and doing the best to ensure it doesn't happen, *because it doesn't fit the Marxist narrative of revolution rather than evolution.* Rather than seeing us as a collection of competing 'victim groups' let us just be a homogenous melting pot of 'different' people who just want to get on with each other.

33 Cultural Marxism has taken this concept of *identity* and twisted and corrupted it. It has used this to pigeon-hole people into controllable groups, by emphasising their form and dismissing their function. It compels people to believe they are defined by their form, whether it is a matter of race, colour, gender inclination, to an extent that they lose any freedom they may have had to express themselves as individuals. Identity has become a bondage rather than something that can benefit people - the

WHO AM I?

ultimate goal of undermining the traditional structures of society and bringing in the extensive State control that Cultural Marxists crave.

The strategy is the same for all of the other artificial 'victim groups' they have created. The 1960s saw the growth of the Civil Rights movement in the USA, in order to improve the status of black people who had been discriminated against for ages. The Civil Rights act in 1964 outlawed segregation in schools, public places and jobs, followed by the Voting Rights Act and the Fair Housing Act. It was all very worthy and it gave us Martin Luther King as a highly respected icon of the movement. This is true social justice in action.

Now we have the movement, *Black Lives Matter* (BLM), formed in 2013 by three female activists in the USA. It supposedly fights racism against black people but seems to only represent a minority of the black community, arguably the more radical and edgy elements. Most black people in the west who have integrated into society have concentrated on careers and calling and *not* identity. The thinking is that, as long as their identity is not creating issues for them, then they would rather dwell on issues of function and purpose. BLM, along with similar groups such as *Antifa* ("anti-fascists" who ironically dress up as fascists and behave like storm-troopers) and *Stop the War Coalition* exist solely to protest and divide and are willing foot soldiers for Cultural Marxism.

You can look and look but, although you will find groups representing such "victims" as Muslims, LGBTQIA, Palestine, the environment, racial minorities and pacifists, you will not find any group defending arguably the most victimised groups in the world today; Christians (particularly in Muslim countries) and, particularly, Jews. Think about *Islamophobia*. It's

WHO AM I?

an artificial construct in order to push a particular narrative and agenda. A phobia is an irrational fear, yet fear of Muslim-inspired terrorism is totally rational, particular as so many of the protagonists are characterised by the statement, *but they seemed like an ordinary quiet family.* There is no Buddhistphobia, Hinduphobia, Christianophobia or Judeophobia, by the way.

If there's any evidence as to the ultimate intentions of this process, then there it is. For Cultural Marxists, the only acceptable narratives for Jews and Christians is either to see them as eternal aggressors (Christians) or arch manipulators (Jews).

At the moment, the 'victim' culture is running amok, with Hollywood and Parliament the current battlefields. For years people have jokingly referred to the producer's 'casting couch', which obviously had a grounding in reality. Now the odious Harvey Weinstein episode has exploded with seemingly every male (heterosexual and homosexual) associated with the film industry who had touched someone else inappropriately twenty years ago is being exposed, with contracts torn up, awards withdrawn and actors airbrushed out of films. Considering that these shenanigans have been known about for years, why is there now such a conveyor belt of 'victims'? The serious stories, of course, need to be told and dealt with and just show what a disgusting place Hollywood is, but one wonders how some may be cashing in empty cheques, unwilling to admit the consensual nature of the 'dastardly deed' as a passport to fame. Cynicism all around, in other words! Surely, like it or not, that's how Hollywood works?

There's a similar story with our politicians, with many chickens coming home to roost. Major figures are being forced to resign on such flimsy pretexts of an 'accidental hand on the knee

WHO AM I?

fifteen years ago' and, although we've always known that our elected representatives have not always been paragons of virtue, we are seeing a fresh explosion of the 'victim' culture that is at the heart of Cultural Marxism.

Everyone seems to be offended about something and our lawyers have never had things so good! We really are a generation of 'snowflakes', particularly if we remember the current atmosphere in our universities, with their 'safe spaces' and lists of do's and don'ts, the *micro-aggressions.*

God forbid if there was ever a serious war! Those grandparents and great-grandparents who have lived through the 1930s and 40s must despair of our rising generation. We have been softened up, our individualism has been clawed away from us as we continue in our lives of 'personal entitlement' and 'human rights', all sanctioned by the Marxist forces that surround us.

34 There's now been time to reflect more since the rally at Trafalgar square, especially in the light of subsequent events in towns and cities throughout the land. A few days after the rally came a spark to ignite the new resolve, to test the unity of what may have been the birth of a new movement in this country. It was a tragedy and it led to further tragedy. A teenage boy of Rwandan origin, though born in Cardiff, went on a killing spree in Southport, knifing to death three innocent girls and maiming many others. This spark, aided by false rumours as to his religious affiliations (i.e. declaring him wrongly as a Muslim), created riots throughout England, something that, at the time of writing nearly two weeks afterwards, has not abated. Our new Prime Minister, Keir Starmer, didn't help by saying that it was 'far right thuggery' at the heart of these disturbances.

WHO AM I ?

This was a significant statement, as here he was providing a link between what is currently happening, to events in the past that *were* a result of 'far right thuggery', though the race riots of the 1980s, in Brixton, Toxteth, Handsworth, Chapeltown and Broadwater Farm were largely fought by young black youths against the police. Unrest at that time was very much initiated on racial lines, but fuelled by poverty and lack of opportunity for the black population. This is to be contrasted to what is happening now, which is not connected to race, but to religion, a *specific* religion, Islam. And it is not an attack on the religion per se, but on those who follow and act on the extreme expressions of it.

A question has to be asked, whether the current unrest is to be placed at the feet of the 'far right'. What is the 'far right'? Is it the same 'far right' as in the days of the National Front and the British National Party, who were most definitely rather nasty racists? Have the definitions changed? I ask this because there is currently a great deal of distress in the same community of people who met peacefully in Trafalgar Square, who were also declared the 'far right' by the media and the government. Yet they were, by and large, ordinary, patriotic citizens. Are they the same people who are now being blamed for the current anti-Muslim disturbances? This is serious, because this can very easily create a rift in UK society that has not been seen for a long, long time. It is all back to our ongoing theme, *identity*. Has a false identity been attached to these people, a convenient classification for the media and politicians to use to create 'an enemy within', in order to follow their own narrative?

35 Again, we return to the question of 'identity'. Let's again look at the average Briton, many of whom were present at the Trafalgar Square rally and were simply there to add their voice to the growing

WHO AM I ?

concerns about where our country is going. They are not thugs or far right or 'nazi scum', just the average person who would have been your average British citizen in outlook up to, say, the 1960s. They are a proud people, patriotic, supporters of (most of) the Royal Family and the traditions that set Britain apart from other nations. They are not, as a whole, racists, certainly not to the same level as earlier generations. Many of their neighbours would be immigrants who have to various degrees assimilated and became proudly 'British'. In fact, in most cases, the defining characteristic and point of connection would be this *Britishness,* rather than their racial or religious backgrounds. They would be most annoyed to be called racists as their only concern is those who are overtly attacking all that they hold dear, whether Islamists or those on the far left, who have turned against their own traditions and heritage. Yet they have been identified as the 'far right' by the media and the politicians, simply because a few among them are hot-headed enough to indulge in thuggery. There are plenty of these on both sides, as actions of the pro-Palestinian demonstrators have shown, yet, in this latter case, it hasn't resulted in everybody on these demos being painted with the same brush and vilified by the authorities. 'Two-tier policing' is a term that is bandied about, not without reason.

Here is a model of what once worked. When the Jews came as immigrants in the late 1800s and early 1900s, fleeing pogroms and persecution, they came as poor, bedraggled folk who spoke no English and had little money. Around 100,000 of them came to London alone. There was already a Jewish community here, having been established over the last 200 years or so and they, rather than the government authorities, looked after their brethren. They met them at the docks, fed them and housed them and helped them find their place in society. They built

WHO AM I ?

hospitals and schools, too. It is worth looking at the ethos of the Jews Free School, at that time the largest school in Europe. They took in these non-English speaking kids and then told them to leave their culture and language at the front door. Only English was spoken at the school and the subjects taught were designed to 'make Englishmen out of them' so that they could become functional citizens when they graduated.

Now compare it with the current model for the largely Muslim refugee population. It should be said that the Muslim community could probably do a lot more to integrate these poor people and help them to become functional members of society. If this was so, and visibly so, then the possibility of resentment by the indigenous population would be minimised and we could have a truly multicultural society. Yet there seem to be elements within Muslim society that don't want this and have their own objectives that may not be in the best interests of those who are already living here. This is the problem, not the actions of the 'far right'. This is what has sparked the riots. The onus is with their own people, aided by the government, to integrate into the society that has *given them refuge.*

36 It is now time to revisit the 'Muslim' situation in our country and the narrative that has been attached to it. The narrative is this; we, the politicians, through our desire to signal our virtues regarding multiculturalism and the need to help the growing refugee crisis, have created a nightmare. We have allowed a large number of people into our country who have no desire to become British citizens but have arrived as a 'fifth column' to spread disruption and worse. These are Muslim zealots and are clearly following a 'narrative' created by Islamists abroad and empowered by those on the far-left over here, as well as some foreign entities who have a clear aim of destabilising our society.

137

WHO AM I?

I have to be clear here, as I was earlier; the majority of Muslims in this country are law-abiding and wish to remain so and simply want to live fruitful and productive lives. What I am suggesting here would seem for some of you, 'conspiracy talk'. But that's an easy excuse because, *what if I am right and it's already too late to do much about it?*

In order to protect the 'narrative' what better way to deflect from this problem than to create scapegoats, focus our attention on those who have woken up to it, perhaps in a clumsy and naïve way (rioting isn't the best way to show displeasure), and labelling them with terms such as 'fascists', 'nazis' or 'far right', so that the Great British Public have ready-made villains to hate. Except, in this case, the villains are you and I. We, dear friends, have become the convenient scapegoats. The sacrificial lambs. We are, apparently, now the 'far right'! The biggest example here is Tommy Robinson, the number one hate figure because he was perhaps the first to wake up to what is going on, utterly despised by the establishment, who have used every way they can to minimise his influence and who has lost family, income and liberty in order to persevere with his message. They would have succeeded if it weren't for social media, particularly Twitter ('X'). I dare you to watch his documentary, *Silenced*. It is a sobering watch to say the least. He is a rough diamond and not to everyone's taste, but focus on the message not the messenger, that is the least we can do. We must not just become followers of an individual, whoever he is. We have become 'Jews', the 'others' who can be painted as bad guys and blamed for all of the mistakes of the establishment. Is it just me? Can we not all see this?

I really hope this works out well and people come to their senses, though I have no confidence in this with the politicians who are currently running our country. Though … and we have

WHO AM I?

to take this seriously ... everyone can change, no-one is irredeemable. There is no space for reconciliation or forgiveness in the Marxist playbook, but who ever thought that they were *completely* in charge?

37 The fact is that there are a growing number of folk who are waking up to this, but how they deal with this has become an issue, because of the adversarial nature of the growing conflict. Peace can't be achieved while there is such conflict in the heart. And this is where, I'm afraid, I feel the need to chart a different course. I don't doubt the sincerity of those leading this counter-movement, but there must be a better way of endearing oneself with the majority of our nation. Sadly, the state of the human heart tells me that this is an ideal that is simply not achievable, unless ...

Let me explain. I am a Christian, by conviction. Many in this movement also claim to have a Christian faith, but I wonder whether it is 'cultural Christianity' we are seeing rather than those with a regenerated heart, which is the hallmark of a true follower of Christ. There was plenty of Christian expression at the Trafalgar Square rally, but to me it seemed to be just a reaction to the pro-Palestinian mobs, a patriotic singing of songs birthed within the heady days of the British Empire and reciting prayers last spoken in school assemblies and the chanting of Jesus' name as if he played as a forward for Arsenal (which in fact he does, for those in the know!) It is a nostalgic Christianity, a comforting reminder of better days, along with memories of street parties, warm beer on village greens and unlocked front doors.

If this movement truly has Jesus at the heart of it, rather than just on the lips, we can safely say that our nation would be

WHO AM I?

utterly transformed, as it was in the 18th Century under John Wesley, the founder of the Methodist Church. Can you imagine a movement that grew to 100,000 strong, totally transforming an England that was ripe for the kind of bloody revolution that swept through America and France at the time and altered the social and moral fabric of society? The parallels to today are chilling, even though Marxism was not around to subvert the culture, but the moral climate had sunk to such a low ebb that something had to give. Thankfully it was God that saved us, not a Tommy Robinson or Keir Starmer or Jeremy Corbyn. Instead, He had John Wesley and George Whitfield, but the revival that ensued flowed through a generation of Christians like them, who were awakened and became a force that totally transformed society. They had completely and utterly surrendered themselves to the Will of God and were used by Him to complete the task. And, believe it or not folks, this is the same God who is still around today … waiting …

At that time the Church was totally ineffectual, corrupt even. It had lost its direction and passion. People considered it irrelevant to their needs and looked elsewhere for direction. There is a marked parallel to today, with the Church in the Twenty-First Century lining up and taking its place among a whole myriad of protest groups and lobbyists, with no status that would compel folk to actually listen to what it is saying. A damp squib, to be honest, riddled with the woke virus and powerless to act as a prophetic mouthpiece for the God who is, I believe, the Creator and Sustainer of the World. Of course, you may disagree with this, but this is my personal view and I offer it to you for your consideration.

Then, in the 18th Century, suddenly people were presented with the life giving and relevant message of Jesus Christ, an offer of sins forgiven, to people who had forgotten – as they have now

WHO AM I?

– exactly what a sin is! They heard this, not in the stifling, alien environments of a church building, but in fields, gardens, public and private spaces. They heard the message where they were, they didn't have to go to find it, it came to them! And it wasn't just a message to mull over and debate, it was actionable and it had the power to transform. And it did. Social change followed, people became aware of the injustices around them and dealt with them. People became ministers of the religion and churches grew in number and effectiveness. This movement became known as a 'Great Awakening' and it touched Britain, central Europe and America. Churches became places of excitement, with great signs and miracles. People fell down under great conviction of their sin and lives were changed at every level of the society of the day.

This excites me because there is ample evidence that God has worked in this way many times in history and not only on the occasion just mentioned. Revivals have sparked in the most unlikely of places among the most unworthy of people. It is the dream of every true Christian that God would break through into the society that surrounds them and show the world a much better way.

38 There's a documentary on BBC iPlayer that is a massive surprise to me because it is totally counter-cultural, not the sort of thing that you'd associate with cozy old Auntie Beeb. It is called *Hypernormalisation* from film-maker Adam Curtis. In around two and a half hours it shows us what has *really* happened in the world over the last 50 years, who *really* calls the shots and runs the world and it is really eye-opening, particularly over the Middle East and what governments and politicians have really got up to there! The conclusion is that no one really knows what's going on, even the politicians and the media gurus, so

141

WHO AM I?

the leaders, financiers, politicians and media have constructed a completely fake version of the world that is accepted as normal because the alternative is too hard to comprehend, that *there is no logic or sense to it all!* This documentary was made around eight years ago, but it feeds right into today's situation, *where no one still seems to know what's going on.*

Now I'm going to get all 'religious' because what we see here is what the Bible calls *the kingdom of the world*. This is the world in which we live but, for Christians, it is not the world in which we operate. Jesus said, *"My kingdom is not of this world"* (John 18:36).

So where is Jesus' kingdom? It lives within our heart and it is what drives us and reassures us and gives us hope whatever is thrown at us. Christians are not *of* the world, but are *in* it and the way we are hopefully going to affect the world is through the truth we represent and the way we allow it to govern the way we live. Sadly, many Christians seem to have forgotten this. It is meant to be their job to make sense of the world through speaking out for God, to show that despite the fact that the world has gone mad, there is *truth* and pattern.

How has this worked out? Badly I would suggest! Here's what it should look like, an invisible Kingdom that connects our spirits together and to the source, God Himself. Our physical bodies may be in the physical world of houses, shopping malls, offices and the corridors of power, but our ambitions, motivations and goals are governed by the spiritual connections as members of this Kingdom.

We are called to be 'salt and light' to the world and to let our lamps shine and, indeed, represent Jesus' likeness, but we are no more part of it than tourists visiting an island paradise. We are not in a rat-race, we should not succumb to the mentality

WHO AM I ?

that insists on the *survival of the fittest*. Out of this thinking comes social abortions (a child would get in the way of my ambitions), abortions of Down Syndrome children (apparently in Iceland this happens in 100% of cases, nothing less than a cull), euthanasia of the elderly (resulting in an early inheritance for family members), ulcers and stress (must work harder, must work harder), marriage breakdowns (too busy earning money to have time to care for a family), fatherless children (can't be tied down, I have a life to live). Here's a sobering picture of the results of such living.

For all can see that the wise die, that the foolish and the senseless also perish, leaving their wealth to others. Their tombs will remain their houses forever, their dwellings for endless generations, though they had named lands after themselves. People, despite their wealth, do not endure; they are like the beasts that perish. This is the fate of those who trust in themselves, and of their followers, who approve their sayings. They are like sheep and are destined to die; death will be their shepherd (but the upright will prevail over them in the morning). Their forms will decay in the grave, far from their princely mansions. (Psalm 49:10-14)

There is a significant difference between these two kingdoms. In the *Kingdom of the World,* your life is lived as in a raging torrent, buffeted on all sides by the winds. Progress is random, seemingly governed by the hands of the Greek deities of luck and fate, but directed overall by society's implementation of evolutionary forces that ensure that only the strong and ruthless flourish and 'looking after number one' is the best way of charting your course through life. Yet the sheer randomness of illness, accident or acts of nature thwart even the mightiest, with no-one guaranteed a truly fulfilled life.

In the *Kingdom of God,* life can still be a struggle and can still be wrenched away from you 'before your time' or ravaged by

WHO AM I?

disease or circumstance, yet the assurance of purpose is there as a constant, even though you may not get the answers you need to make sense of it. The guarantee is of a glorious future, but not necessarily of a trouble-free present.

Our call in the world should be one of *pro-action*, not reaction. What do I mean by this? Our Christian sub-culture is good in what it calls *relevance* and *engagement*. Dan Brown writes the *Da Vinci Code* and twenty Christian writers write rebuttals of it. Something happens in politics and umpteen Christian bloggers, writers and columnists tells us *"What Jesus would do ..."* according to what their particular Jesus, governed by their flavour of Christianity, tells them. We seem to have the answer to all the foibles and strains of living in the 21st Century and are quite willing to add our voice to the hundreds of other voices responding to the same triggers according to their worldview.

39 The problem is that there are as many flavours of Christian opinion as there are flavours of political opinion. There is no one authoritative voice. No wonder no one is listening to us! In fact, our stance on the issues of the day is key to the way we are perceived by the world at large. We are not to be just one voice of many, commentary with a "Christian twist". We have *the* answers, we need to act as if we really understand that and have the authority to back it up. After all, Jesus has given us the authority to heal and work miracles in his name, we also have the authority to *speak in his name.* So why don't we?

Fear ... of loss of credibility and acceptance. That's what drives many Christian commentators, particularly those of a liberal 'persuasion' who, *when push turns to shove,* often offer views on social matters closer to their secular counterparts than many of their Christian *brothers and sisters.* How on earth can we be

144

WHO AM I?

consistent in our witness in the world if we offer such a range of opinions? I say this because I am tarred with the same brush, I can equally be faulted by my liberal Christian brothers and sisters for not agreeing with them.

On many issues they are not going to get *us*. That doesn't make them right and us wrong, it simply means that we have a clash of Kingdoms here. This means that we are only truly going to communicate clearly when there's a meeting of spirits as there will never be a full meeting of minds. This is because *our source is the Bible and theirs isn't*. If they don't accept the Bible then they are never going to accept our views. The only honest approach is to make this clear and to tell them that, as Christians, that is what defines us and we would not be true to ourselves if we compromised this position. You may even get grudging respect, perhaps more than you realise, as admitted by Daily Mail columnist, Sarah Vine, in a column (12th October 2016) about Christian campaigner Mary Whitehouse:

"When I was growing up in the Eighties, Mary Whitehouse was a figure of fun. With her horn-rimmed spectacles, stiff hair and collection of prim hats, she exemplified everything that was repressive about the old order. The more she carped on about traditional values and 'dirty' plays, the more we rolled our eyes and determined to ignore her. She was a joyless, stuffy, stick-in-the-mud suburban prude, whose very name became a byword for laughable, old-fashioned priggery — so much so that she even had a late-night BBC alternative comedy show, The Mary Whitehouse Experience, named after her. Just imagine the smug self-congratulation of whoever came up with that name. How clever! How ironic! How brilliantly post-modern! Now, it turns out, we were wrong, and Mary — object of a thousand cheap jokes — was right all along. Not only right, but perhaps even a visionary. Or, at least, so says the man who helped thwart her crusade against obscenity in the Eighties, Jeremy Hutchinson QC, now 101. Hutchinson made a mockery of Whitehouse's

WHO AM I?

private prosecution against theatre director Michael Bogdanov, whose 1982 staging of Howard Brenton's play The Romans In Britain depicted a violent male rape ..."

She summarises with this telling statement:

"I'll say. If we had been able to suspend just a smidgeon of our liberal snobbery towards Mary to take in even a tenth of what she was telling us, we might well be living in a better world today. Perhaps if we had listened a little more and sniggered a little less, we might have understood that the boundaries she fought so hard to protect were not repressive — they were precious."

We need more Mary Whitehouses but there don't seem to be any around. We need to speak out with authority and certainty, even on contentious topics. Unfortunately, the time is fast approaching when plain speaking is going to get us in trouble, but this is not without precedent if we read the stories of the early Church, or the steadfast Christian believers throughout history who have spoken the truth whatever the personal outcome – prison, banishment, even death.

Pro-action compels us to proclaim the Gospel even when it is 'out of season'. It is not about being popular or even relevant because *the reality of sin in the human heart* is not a trendy topic or one to attract an attentive audience at dinner parties or soirees. John Wesley was relentless in presenting this topic, as he traipsed around the English countryside on horseback, whether or not people wanted to hear it. How many of us Christians have a similar call on our life but are not fulfilling it out of fear or impracticability? If we are pro-active we are out there creating the agenda, not responding to it along with countless others and therefore lost in the crush.

WHO AM I?

4O But, dear friends, it is time to get personal. Every journey starts with a single step and rather than bemoan the state of society and how we are making a complete mess of it, the first place we need to visit is … ourselves.

And this brings me back to the subject of your search, our *identity*. For Christians this is an easy one, *our identity is in Jesus*. I say 'easy', as it is on paper, but, in actuality, it's hard, perhaps the hardest thing. That's because he set the highest possible standard.

And we all, who with unveiled faces contemplate the Lord's glory, are being transformed into his image with ever-increasing glory, which comes from the Lord, who is the Spirit. (2 Corinthians 3:18)

Our identity should therefore be precious for us, but not our past identity, defined by race, culture or family, but our future identity, when we will be presented to Jesus … *as a radiant church, without stain or wrinkle or any other blemish, but holy and blameless.* (Ephesians 5:27)

This is a message for those who are men and women of God. This may or may not be relevant for you, Derek and Dawn, but I really believe it offers the only solution and you would do well to … follow the evidence!

It is time for Christians to wake up. We have slept through this for long enough. We are a mighty army, but we don't know it, because our weapons are not made of steel, but of prayer. We don't march or fight on our feet, but on our knees. Prayer is the Christian's vital breath and one that, in our arsenal of weapons, is often the most powerful in battle with a culture that has lost its moral compass.

And that's all I'm going to say for now, dear folk. Yes, this has

WHO AM I?

been long and perhaps difficult to read in places, but I hope it has been useful. Of course, it is all written from my perspective and perhaps your perspective is still a work-in-progress. All I can say that my viewpoint, as a Christian, is the only one that makes sense of the world and, most importantly, gives me hope for the future.

With much love, Dave.

WHO AM I?

You will find the following resources useful:

BOOKS by Steve Maltz

Available from good bookshops or https://www.saltshakers.com

Now Everything Changes

Derek and Dawn's first adventure, leading them into an understanding of the causes and effects of antisemitism, particularly in the wake of the war in Gaza. This is followed by looking at the implications and relevance of this to our own lives.

Into the Lion's Den

This ground-breaking book explores the unseen force that is behind the current explosion in the areas of political correctness, 'victim groups', the 'nanny state', 'naming and blaming' and issues of gender, race and religion.

Noise

This little book sifts through the 'noise' of political correctness, victim culture, new age spirituality, militant atheism and so on and uncovers where real truth may be found. Suitable for Christians or non-Christians, this book makes sense of the madness that surrounds us

Awake

An encouragement for us to break out of the confusion that surrounds us all

Icebreaker

How can Christians reach the world when our culture has us by the throat with the collective madness of victim mentality, the stretching of truth to fit dubious agendas and the fear of being cancelled through "unacceptable" speech?

WHO AM I?

PODCAST

Available on Spotify, Apple, Amazon and YouTube

Is there Fudge on Mars?

Yes, it is real and so are 'Podcast Steve' and 'Podcast Dave', with their sidekick David. It covers the themes of this book and a lot more. You will find it on all of the major podcast platforms, as well as their ministry website at *www.saltshakers.com.*